Of Farming and Classics

OF FARMING & CLASSICS

A Memoir

DAVID GRENE

University of Chicago Press
Chicago & London

The University of Chicago Press, Chicago 60637
The University of Chicago Press, Ltd., London
© 2007 by The University of Chicago
All rights reserved. Published 2007
Paperback edition 2008
Printed in the United States of America

17 16 15 14 13 12 11 10 09 08   3 4 5 6

ISBN-13: 978-0-226-30801-2 (cloth)
ISBN-13: 978-0-226-30802-9 (paper)
ISBN-10: 0-226-30801-4 (cloth)
ISBN-10: 0-226-30802-2 (paper)

Brendan Kennelly's poem "In a Drizzly Light" is included by kind
permission of the author. Some parts of this memoir were previously
published in *Ideas Matter: Essays in Honor of Conor Cruise O'Brien* (Dublin:
Poolbeg, 1998).

Library of Congress Cataloging-in-Publication Data

Grene, David.
    Of farming & classics : a memoir / David Grene.
        v.   cm.
    Includes bibliographical references and index.
    Contents: The beginning—Origins—Family—Dublin—The theater—
Tipperary—Schools—Trinity College—Vienna—Return to Dublin : Ria
Mooney—America—University of Chicago—Farming—Riding to hounds.
    ISBN 0-226-30801-4 (cloth : alk. paper)
    1. Grene, David.   2. Classicists—United States—Biography.   I. Title.   II. Title:
Of farming and classics.
    PA85.G646A3   2007
    880.9—dc22
    [B]
                                                        2006012465

⊗ The paper used in this publication meets the minimum requirements
of the American National Standard for Information Sciences—
Permanence of Paper for Printed Library Materials, ANSI Z39.48-1992.

Title Page: David Grene on the Midway at the University of Chicago,
c. 1950. Photo by James Stricklin.

Contents

In a Drizzly Light

Brendan Kennelly

February 1996
In a drizzly light outside the Abbey Theatre
David Grene is talking of ancient Greece,
no, not talking

revealing
in that calm attentive smiling style of his
the ways of gods and goddesses
the ways of words and images

Cities   rivers   mountains   sacrifices.

Listening
in the drizzly light, I hear him
opening
Cavan   Athens   Dublin   Chicago
small hills   actors   lovers   passionate minds.

I'm in the company of one
who loves adventure
and will pursue it with that laughing brio
to the moment of discovery.

Love is what he finds.

Foreword

I arrived in Chicago in 1992, and was asked to be the chair of the Committee on Social Thought a couple of years later. So I only knew David Grene during the last decade of his long, interesting life, and knew him mostly from the perspective of a colleague and as the chair of the Committee, an institution he cared so much about and did so much to nourish and sustain.

I should say first, however, that I count myself primarily a student of David Grene, but in a somewhat different sense than so many others over so many decades. I was a student in the traditional sense, too. I sat in on some of his classes and read his work and translations, and I learned an enormous amount listening to him at that most interesting and valuable Committee event, our discussions of student Fundamentals exams. But he was also a teacher in a more personal sense, and I want to say something about what he taught me.

Anyone who simply knows how to listen can learn a lot from any great *éminence grise*, a thoughtful, wise elder who has lived through interesting times and seen a lot; someone on whom nothing is lost. And as this memoir shows, that was certainly true of David's rich, varied, and passionate life, and anyone who ever met him knew immediately that he was a man on whom very little, if anything, was lost. He certainly knew some interesting people. One of the first stories he told me at our gin and cheeseburger lunches at Jimmy's (the closest Hyde Park can get to a pub) is recounted in these pages. It was a hilarious yarn about carrying a fan letter from Felix Frankfurter (whom he had gotten to know at Harvard) to Harpo Marx (this must have been in the late thirties; David had been offered a job doing some script doctoring in Hollywood), and of giving the letter to a greatly impressed and overjoyed Harpo at a party. He also told a wonderful long story of a bizarre dinner with Jack Warner and the Lunts. And of course a "farmer classicist" is bound to have seen life from many angles.

But in a more personal sense, David was invaluable to me because in the ten years I knew him, he simply embodied the entire history of the Committee on Social Thought, and so he functioned for me as the Conscience of the Committee. Since there is only one Committee on Social Thought and since, I discovered, many things widely believed about it are false, it was not easy to get one's bearings in those early years. If, during a meeting, I would see David getting uncomfortable or impatient (and you could always tell), I knew we must be going in the wrong direction and that I could call on him to set us straight, which he invariably did. And if we got tired of the confusions that our do-it-yourself graduate program would cause and found ourselves tempted by the illusory solution of rules and regulations and deadlines, David would remind us that we were here to be different, and should resist being pulled toward the norm. He could always be counted on to keep the Committee on the straight and narrow path, which in the Committee's case meant insuring that we were never on any straight and narrow path.

More substantively, I only dimly understood when I arrived what it really means to ignore—completely, fiercely, deliberately to ignore—disciplinary regulations and credentials, to follow your ideas wherever they lead you, and to work only on books and ideas that you care deeply about, in whatever way it makes sense to you to read and think about them, however the academy has decided to organize itself. I know that I have never met anyone before or since whose relation to books was so passionate and so extraordinarily independent, marked by such integrity and love. So, it was from him most of all that I learned I finally had permission, really and truly, to escape the often arbitrary organization of the academy, or at least to try to manage it on my own terms, not its.

Everyone who knew David can cite many examples of this dedication and independence of spirit. When I first became chair, I was astonished to discover that, for quite a long time after his official retirement, David, into his eighties by this point, had been teaching four courses a year for the Committee on a completely voluntary basis, just out of love for teaching, for his students, for the books taught, and for the conversations that such teaching produced. He also conducted several tutorials with students who wanted to read Greek texts with him. And he would have continued to do so, indefinitely; he had never mentioned to me that this service was unpaid. I learned it only by chance. Of course, we corrected the problem immediately and paid David the maximum we could for those courses, but I know of few other such demonstrations of integrity and commitment to students by so-called retired faculty, a phrase that was completely irrelevant in David's case.

I certainly learned something about students, too. I noticed that everyone who studied with David seemed not just to appreciate him but to cherish him as a life-long friend and mentor. He didn't of course take on every student who wanted to study with him; he had his own standards and he applied them consistently. (I found this out the hard way in my first quarter at Chicago by making a timid remark about Greek at a seminar of his that I was attending. David asked me to come see him the next day, immediately produced the Greek passage I had mouthed off about, and, smiling, asked me to "go on some more about what you were saying last night." I had had a few years of Greek in graduate school, but was nowhere near the same league—or universe—of David and his students, but in a great stroke of luck I happened to have studied the passage before, so was able to stumble through it well enough for David not to write me off his list. But it was a good lesson in the seriousness with which he took claims about the Greek language.)

But again these standards weren't ideological or personal, as they often are in graduate school. I have met many people who, it seemed to me, became who they are because of David, but I have never met any "Greneans." He founded no schools or sects. And this can't be an accident, as anyone who has taught knows. It meant he had mastered the most delicate part of the art of teaching—the art of inspiring without dominating.

David ended up not just teaching students but believing in them in a way I have never seen with another teacher in my thirty years of doing this; many times I saw that it resulted in the students believing in themselves. It meant, for example, a very great deal to me that he believed in me as chair of the Committee, so I have some sense of the benefit, the great lift, that students enjoyed as a result of his faith. It was something you had to earn, but once earned, you never lost it.

Likewise, he taught all of us to take chances with students. Every year at admissions meetings, David would find in the large pile one or two applicants who would normally not have made the final cut. He had noticed something in one of their essays and statements of purpose and usually was able to argue us into admitting them. And he was almost always right—the student was a perfect fit for us, would thrive here in a way not evident in the transcript or test score. This required a risk, and David was always willing to take it and to lead the way for the rest of us.

That's a very great deal of indebtedness to be thankful for, and in my case, besides sadness at David's death, and sympathy for David's family and very close friends, I am also simply very deeply grateful for having had the privilege of knowing him and learning from him. David was the last living link with the giants of the original Committee and its first full generation. I hope that we at Chicago will be worthy of what he and others created. We won't see his like again.

Robert Pippin

The Beginning

I am quite sure that from my early days—say eight or nine—
the strongest sense of pleasure I enjoyed was in watching or
tending animals and in trying to interchange the content of
books into real facts of my own life.

The books were most often history—the old simpleminded
history books of those days with dates of the kings and moral
judgments on each one, and battles lost and won. I had an
objection to fairy stories, as not real, but I had the absurd
habit of trying to change the course of history and imagine
that my heroes, for instance the Stuart kings, had won, that
James II had recovered his kingdom, or that Bonnie Prince
Charlie had driven out George II in 1745. But there were also
novels to delight me—Walter Scott and Harrison Ainsworth
and G. A. Henty, and again I frequently retold myself the
stories, making the necessary corrections to suit my notion of
how things *ought* to have come out. I suppose that the facts
of history still remained facts for me even after I had altered
them, and the destiny of characters in fiction still preserved
their lives since they were projected from the printed page
anyhow, and my putting speeches into their mouths or ideas
into their heads still did not violate their ultimate existence
as their authors had given them to me. It was just that some

other things had happened to them that the writers did not know about.

Perhaps it was only in poetry that I rejoiced in just what I read, and that was because the sound and the rhythm captivated me. Those needed no admixture of how I wanted "real" life to be.

I have always, for as long as I could recollect anything, been a happy visitor at zoos, but from the age of seven or eight I tried to form small zoo-like communities for myself—white mice, guinea pigs, rabbits, and a hedgehog that I captured, though like all hedgehogs I have ever known he managed to escape fairly soon. I know too that I wanted mostly to watch my pets. I did not want to handle them especially, and so though I had a dog or two to raise, dogs were never exactly what I liked best. When I could watch the mice and guinea pigs and others, and feed them, and come to know what their community was like, I was very content. Certainly, this kind of management was the complement to my obsession with reality in books, as opposed to the fantastic quality of fairy stories. Animals are undeniably real, and so are their lives when you can watch them all together.

The conclusion of these childish peculiarities has apparently been that from my early twenties, I have been a farmer and a university teacher of Greek and Latin literature. I suppose that with slightly different influences, I might have been a teacher of English or some other modern language, but from the age of ten, something latched my child's imagination to Greek. Very soon afterward—and for that I am everlastingly grateful to my first Greek teacher, of whom more later—I met with Homer and then Herodotus, and this settled my devotion to Greek forever afterward. At the beginning, I am afraid, it was nothing more profound than the strange alphabet and the knowledge that those letters, unknown to most readers, spoke to me intelligibly.

The pets were gradually replaced by my care of my mother's hens, which she started to keep in our back garden, and the management factor in me increased in importance, and drew me closer to the farming which I eventually adopted. This latter might never have happened but that I had cousins who had two farms

David, about age five, holding horses on his cousin's farm in Tipperary

in Tipperary, and as a child I used to go there in summer, and more and more afterward; and though at twenty I had no idea how I would ever come to be able to buy a farm, I was bent on doing so. Mine was a thoroughly practical concern. I intensely despised what I heard called "gentleman farmers." I wanted to do the farming tasks myself—the milking and feeding and finally, when I got the chance, which was not till I had emigrated to the United States, to do the plowing and work of cultivation.

Similarly, or so it seems to me still, I needed to read the novels and poems I loved, and when I had thoroughly grasped them or learned them by heart, I wanted to talk about them with others like myself. From this to teaching is only a very small leap. It is certainly the way I want to teach still. I have never felt concerned with the methods of understanding literature or philosophy. It is the particularity of the book, or the particular poem that concerns me. The only outside matter to take account of is how it stands related to the rest of the author's writings.

Why am I sharing what can at least pass for a connected, if incomplete narrative of my life? There does have to be, of course, someone else for whom one writes besides oneself. One cannot really know one's own face better for looking at it in a mirror, because of the self-consciousness of that look. The obvious answer as to an audience is one's family. Yes, this is written for my family. But not only the family. Maybe the oddity of the conjunction of my two interests, farming and classical literature, is the reason for describing the way I went. I rather doubt it, for so odd it isn't, though a little unusual. Maybe the book is due to a warmth of feeling for the two professions, some perhaps misguided zeal for two causes not very high on the world's popularity list. That is nearer it, I think. Or maybe it is just a rechewing of the grateful joys of the past, and sometimes of their opposites. I know that many people believe in the genuine isolation of the past: let it bury its own dead, its successes, and its failures; continuity is the supreme illusion. I have never been able to see it like that.

Origins

There are two framed documents hanging in my study on my Cavan farm which are my closest link with real history, and also the most evocative. The first of them is nearly five feet long and gaudy with gold, black, and red coloring. It traces the Grene family from its possible origin in Kent in the twelfth century till the time the first Grene came to Ireland, which happened in 1609. This family tree itself was drawn up by the then king-at-arms, William Camden (and as such signed by him) with that date, 1609. No one knows why that particular Grene became interested in getting his family tree authenticated at that date. Possibly because King James I had given this George Grene a grant of Irish land in County Kilkenny. Again, no one knows why the king should have given him the land in Ireland. Perhaps the Grenes had lent the king money, and this was in the nature of a repayment. The Grene family was then Catholic, and without some other very strong claims on the royal attention, they would have hardly been so favored. King James had been brought up a Presbyterian, and though he was aware that there were many loyalists who were Catholic, the Gunpowder Plot of 1605, designed to blow up the entire Parliament and the King, would hardly have made him particularly favorable to someone qua

Catholic. Camden was also the king-at-arms when he gave Shake-speare his coat of arms sometime in the 1590s, and some people have linked this also with an acquisition of some extra property.

The construction of the thing is fascinating. Most families till, say, the middle nineteenth century, had coats of arms which they stamped on the doors of their carriages and elsewhere on their various pieces of equipment. The king-at-arms traced these coats of arms through the generations, and each generation contributed new features from events of their day in which they had partic-ipated. Thus, ours has a very prominent cross to commemorate participation in the Crusades. The final coat—that is, the one made up by the king-at-arms at the request of the member of the family—involved creating an amalgam of all the special designs, put together with traditional colors and patterns. Hence, notes like "azure upon a field d'or." The names of the generations of Grenes are given in Latin, with occasional additions such as *eques auratus*, "gilded horseman," which means he had the order of knighthood.

It is natural to be a bit skeptical. I wonder, for instance, how possible it was for Camden or his assistants literally to run down the names of all the family members for as far back as three to four hundred years. I wonder, even more, if such efforts could be made and made successfully, how could the time and energy possibly be commensurate with any likely payment—even if we know that the costs of establishing the family tree were high.

Yet, there are signs of some serious trying for accuracy. The further back you go, the more often you find *nomine ignoto*, "this man's (Christian) name is unknown," and even more frequently, after listing a son, his father's marriage is noted as *uxor eius ig-nota*, "wife unknown." Unless the job was taken seriously, I hardly think the maker of the tree would patently admit ignorance, in-stead of inventing a name in either instance. But the piece of evi-dence that seems to me to give the strongest sense of an attempt at accuracy is something else. Originally, the Grenes were not Grenes at all but Nortons. It is the Nortons who were in the Cru-sades and the Nortons who are traceable to the reign of Stephen. About the end of the fourteenth or beginning of the fifteenth century, there was a Grene with the added note *filius naturalis,* though for a couple of generations the entry reads "Grene alias Norton." This was about Chaucer's time, and the spelling "grene" occurs in Chaucer. (Names like Grene, White, Brown, etc., have in various countries been taken when the state authorities forced their previously unidentifiable citizens to have a new signification. Those who took names from colors, or from trades like Smith or Baker, did not want or did not dare to call themselves after a family of real distinction.) From this time on there were Grenes, and for several generations they carry the Norton arms with the *bordure compony,* a particular design around the border of the coat which like a bend (bar) sinister indicates bastardy. After what was either a conventional or perhaps only a respectable interval, this was dropped (presumably by order of William Camden or his assistant), and the Grenes quietly emerge with the Norton arms. I don't know what happened to the Nortons; maybe the family died out. But if there had not been a very serious and concerned search after accuracy, it would surely have been tempting and certainly less likely to give offense for the searcher to skip the awkwardness of the *filius naturalis,* and have invented an original Grene with no dishonorable origin noted. So I am inclined to believe that this is a serious effort at historical accuracy, and that when the records were more numerous, it was possible to examine them more easily than I would have imagined.

My grandfather had a passionate interest in the pedigree, and on his own continued it from the original George Grene of 1609 till his own time. He died in 1910. Though his version of the pedigree is not nearly as sensational in its coloring (and, of course, of much less value as a historical document), running only in plain black and green lines, it has for me a special interest, because the seventeenth, eighteenth, and nineteenth centuries of Irish history are so close to my heart. My grandfather also very obligingly wrote a longish piece on the family, drawing on sources no longer available. In his day, there were many records kept in Thomastown, County Kilkenny, where the Grenes had originally been given their land. These records were mostly transferred to the Four

Courts in Dublin in the early years of the twentieth century and were largely destroyed in the burning of the Four Courts during an episode of the Civil War in 1922. One of the Grenes was hanged by Cromwell about 1650, and so presumably had been serving as an officer in the Royalist army. Another fought at the Boyne for King James II in 1689. Thereafter his sons and grandsons, some of them anyway, fought in the French army and, according to my grandfather's account, one of them fought at Dettingen in 1742 against King George II. Apparently some of the Grenes, brothers or otherwise, stayed on in Ireland, for my grandfather found the names of land farmed by them at the time that Sylvester Grene was at Dettingen.

Of course, that such documents should arouse emotion and pride is a bit absurd. Every son of Adam has ancestors, even if they do not figure in family trees. It would be also more pardonable to feel these emotions if the ancestors for generations had played a prominent part in the great events. I cannot really say that for the Grenes. Even those with the destinies that seem violent, like the man who was hanged by Cromwell or they who fought at the Boyne or Dettingen, were doing quite typical things for the minor gentry that they were. When I knew that I was being overpowered by the family tree, I was secretly pleased by the scurrilous comment of my aunt Jessie, well known for her acid tongue. She said that she had never heard of anything unusual done by these ancient Grenes except that she had heard of one of them so poor (and so greedy) that he had given the family tree as security (I am glad to say temporarily) for a leg of mutton.

There were also some matters of the greatest concern to myself, exclusively recorded in my grandfather's account. Somewhere in the early eighteenth century, Patrick Grene married twice. His first wife was a lady called Elizabeth Russell, his second, Susan Colpys. By his first wife, among other children, he had an eldest son, Sylvester. This is my direct ancestor. By his second, he had another family, and these are the so-called cousins with whom we have always had the kindest relations. I do not know at what time the Grenes migrated from County Kilkenny to Tipperary, but by the early nineteenth century the Grenes of Patrick's second family already owned Cappamurra there, with a lot of land and a most beautiful old house. Another of them, Nicholas Biddulph Grene, owned the land of what has since been called Grenepark, and built there in 1826 another medium-sized but splendidly dignified Regency place. At that time my great-grandfather George Grene apparently owned a large farm at Clonmel, about twelve miles off, and used to ride over to breakfast with Nicholas Biddulph when Grenepark was building.

Now comes the matter that interested me so, especially when I was a child. The intimacy between the two branches of the family was then as now very close, unexpectedly so since the "cousin-ship" is a very formal title for a very distant relation if one figures out the range of years and the half nature of the kinship anyway. So far both branches of the family seem to have been about equally well-to-do, and both lived off the land. Then my great-grandfather George married a Scotch lady who was Protestant and turned Protestant himself, sometime about 1830.

There had never been a Protestant Grene before, and what-ever uncomfortable fates had befallen the members of the family, all had happened because they remained obdurately Catholic. It is paradoxical that my great-grandfather turned when Catholic emancipation was already a fact, and his conversion clearly made little difference in his prospects. Anyway, the Scotch lady had money and did not like the country, and the two went up to Dublin and bred up most of their children to be lawyers and doctors and businessmen. Among them, my grandfather became an officer of the Royal Irish Constabulary and eventually Dis-trict Inspector. This looks well on paper and, in fact, was a fairly important position, for there were only about fifteen of them in Ireland. It is now the custom to dispraise the RIC as harsh and tyrannical, especially in their function as the official opponent of the rising nationalism. It is rather hard to get at many facts about this, though as police against antigovernmentalists, they are hardly likely to have been very merciful. My grandfather was very badly injured in the Belfast riots in the middle eighties, and a few years afterward was retired and went to live in Dublin. There is an ominous note on his record describing him as a "zealous, perhaps at times, an overzealous officer." I know his photograph well, and the face has always looked to me quite brutal.

Meanwhile, the other Grenes stuck to Cappamurra and Grenepark. They sent their children to good Catholic schools; some of them became priests, monks, or nuns. Mostly, they continued to farm. By the middle twenties, they were at least in fairly comfortable terms to face the depression. My side of the family, well represented by professionals and businesspeople, managed in about one hundred years to lose all their money. My father was an accountant in the Sun Insurance office in Dublin, a job that was got for him because he had an uncle who was a director of the company in London, and it was always thought that some of his influence would push my father further up the tree. It never did. He remained an accountant on a very middling salary for a very middling job, which he was far from liking.

I was, I know, a sentimental child, rather lonely and self-absorbed. History was my principal form of reading entertainment. To my young mind, looking at the family tree, and especially that part of it drawn up by my grandfather and bearing on the eighteenth and nineteenth centuries, it seemed compellingly clear that the old way of living on the land was the right one. The city was at best mildly interesting, and more often tawdry. My great-grandfather had taken the wrong road, and I myself could see the results of it. Instead of looking after land and animals, we were cooped up in this little terrace house with none of the joy I used to experience in what were merely holidays spent in Tipperary every year. When I was on either of the two farms, I was incessantly and delightfully busy milking, feeding the animals, learning the ways of grass and grazing. Ireland generally is a great grazing country to such a degree that I have very often heard farmers say that the worst thing you ever did was to turn the ground upside down on the furrow slice. Every day's occupation was a new occasion for happiness. I still read as I did in Dublin, but, of course, for shorter periods and fewer books. But in those days of long ago, I already began to find that the one pursuit balanced the other. My joy in books and the way I learned were enhanced by the work of the farm and vice versa. I have found that confirmed and strengthened in the years since. It is perhaps not very good for one to spend one's time working incessantly physically, but it emphatically is most risky for someone to live off thoughts, expressing them and writing them down, with no ballast in manual work.

As I watched the family move from their self sufficiency (shown in the bare records of the generations) to my father's dreary ledgers at the office, and the debts and pettiness of that home life, I knew what I knew and I knew what I was going to do, if it could be done at all—get back on the land. There was no possibility of having one of the Tipperary farms. They were already preempted by a host of their own little native-born Grenes. Somehow, I would have to buy a farm. Then, I had not the slightest idea of how it could be done. As it turned out, by following my intellectual interests, getting a university job, and going to America to teach, I managed somehow with infinite scraping and gambling on chances, first to buy an American farm, and afterward to sell it and buy a farm in Wicklow, so that I could teach one-half of the year in America and farm for the rest in Ireland. Finally, when I left that first Irish farm in Wicklow which was later taken over by my eldest son, I bought another for myself in Cavan. These were all smallish farms—the last one, with fifty acres, being the smallest. But that suited me. I have never wanted to depute the work to someone else as long as I was on the place myself. When I did not do the work myself, it lost half its fascination. I was helped tremendously in achieving this ambition by pure luck. From 1940 to 1960, land was dirt cheap in America and Ireland. Why everywhere today the cost of it has outrun what you can make from it, I do not quite understand. Perhaps, there is everywhere some obscure feeling that things might come to a pass when you had no security of food and shelter unless you owned the means of both. Perhaps, that is even true. In any case, I would never have had the money to buy these farms if I had had to try thirty years later in each instance.

Another by-product of my study of the family tree was the conviction that the old religion was also the best. The Catholicism of the pre-great-grandfather vintage was the right sort of faith. In the light of it, hadn't they taken the right side through the centuries—shades of the Stuart cause? But the logical outcome of that would have been to turn Catholic, and that I somehow would not do; mostly, I think, because this meant turning back on something I already was, a sort of Protestant. I have always had some misgivings about the idea of conversion anyway, as indeed about any very radical shifts of inner conviction. So though the lesson of trying to buy a farm came through and bore fruit, the other history-supported position did not. I suppose that there is a kind of conservatism in both decisions.

3

Family

My parents' house was on Belmont Avenue in Dublin, just three miles from the Pillar, which was always known as the center of the city. The Pillar commemorated Nelson's victory at Trafalgar. That was the starting point for all the trams, except such as were linked with lines going north. I remembered Number 12 with joy when I read the cries in *Ulysses*, "Start, Palmerston Park" and can still identify the numbers of almost all the tram routes. This has since been made easier, because with an unexpected attack of nostalgia the Dublin centralized bus company has transferred the old tram numbers to the buses, except of course for the many new ones that now connect Dublin not only with the suburbs but with Enniskerry and such towns twelve or more miles away.

Belmont Avenue was a series of smallish houses built about the middle of the nineteenth century, but really directly patterned, though on a small scale, on the typical eighteenth-century house. They were modest, but not exactly unassuming. Nowadays they have become expensive and much sought-after. This interesting development happened because now there are miles and miles of monotonous bungalows and ranch-type homes reaching out toward all the small country towns and along the seacoast to Dalkey and Killiney. Against

13

this sort of self-effacement, Belmont Avenue and its like appear interesting to a strong minority of city dwellers, and the prices of all its houses have gone up. This was an area of small houses, small shops, a feeling of personal relationship in everything one did—that was the pattern of my parents' life. For the twenty years of my growing up, they always had the same grocery, the same butcher. Everyone ran up bills; and credit, in limited amounts, was the basis of all our trade. There was an agreed convention that if you owed, say, sixty pounds, you continually diminished it by payments of about twenty or thirty, but its final liquidation always waited for the demise of shopkeeper or customer. I don't think I ever heard of anyone intentionally or even unintentionally bilking one's particular shop.

I still do not know whether this system was good or bad economically. I do know what the mental atmosphere was like. It was a curious blend of a somewhat enforced trust on one side, and something like uneasy gratitude on the other.

One personal result of this system, which was perhaps more peculiar than I thought it, was that from very early I had a precocious knowledge of where we stood financially. When I was ten to twelve, I would be sent to do "messages" as it was called then— that is, to buy butter or bread from the grocery, or fish or rabbits or meat from the butcher. I grew horribly sensitive to the small signs of unwillingness or hesitation on the part of shopkeepers and asked my mother about it. Gradually, I really do not know why, she told me nearly all the sums we owed and how they were being (one hoped) decreased. I suppose it would be reasonable to expect that such a beginning would make me either a reckless spendthrift, in opposition, or a prudent and cautious adult in dealing with money. As far as I can see, it has not done exactly either, but it certainly has had a very striking effect. I developed then, and have never managed to rid myself of it since, a capacity to pick up the knowledge of what everything costs in a given society. It is somehow related to a similar knack of invariably knowing the time without the use of a watch. They are both neurotic tricks, I think, but they have their uses. I am extravagant, more so than is reasonable, but the prices of the items continue to haunt my mind and do some sort of a balancing act in my head. If I spend this, I cannot spend money on that. It becomes a continual game of choice. Any temptation to live on a sensible policy of spending just so much and putting away more has always been easy to resist. The real crunch comes in the case of attractive major choices. Shall I venture on that, and half starve in between the choice and its achievement or failure? Luckily, I seem to have been able to buy all three farms I have owned on a very small income for such an investment. All three were very difficult investments to make.

Though nagged by debts, my parents possessed a huge gift of cheerfulness, and even joy in living. They were great gardeners, and had a nice small back garden devoted to flowers aside from what was then called the allotments—vacant land that could be rented very cheaply to grow vegetables. My father was a real expert at this, and he loved doing it. He was a very good carpenter too, and kept our house in a satisfactory state of repair entirely on his own. (There was a kind of agreement between himself and a most extremely mean landlord that the rent was very low as long as the landlord was never asked to foot the bill for any repairs.) He also built a greenhouse and a toolshed in the garden, and he was very good-natured later when he remarked that the space in the toolshed was nearly useless to him because it was occupied by my white mice, guinea pigs, rabbits, and hedgehogs. These were the delight of my leisure time between the ages of six and eleven, and after that they vanished in favor of my mother's flock of hens. But I have not forgotten my gratitude to my father who, in spite of his resentment of my pets and his own very tepid feelings about any kind of animal, built me cages for the offending beasts. I also remember my excitement at breeding blue mice. You can do this by crossing pure black and pure white mice. The progeny come out a genuine light blue and these used to sell at three months old for six pence rather than three pence. I realized that the blue mice were going to other small boys and girls as pets and that the three-penny whites were going for lab work—both kinds being of course sold to the pet shops and by the pet shops again. I cannot say I was overwhelmed with unhappiness about the future of the white mice. Even then, I thought that the labs were their destiny on the market. If I could keep them reasonably happy as they were growing up, they were like all other animals: they had their lot in life. I can now see that those white mice did have a valuable function in the society. I really did not see it then, but my hardness of heart starts with the idea that domestic animals live for man's use and pleasure, but he must give them a fair show on the way.

My parents were both kind and generous to me, considering that I had very few interests in common with them. Neither of them read anything that mattered—my father enjoying detective novels and my mother "nice" stories like those of Ethel M. Dell.

My father had great value for modernity and progress, and used to tell me that I would live to see horses only in zoos. He combined this with a curious belief (that I have found in odd places elsewhere) that all the improvements of the modern world—cars, telephones, radio—had been invented thousands of years ago by the Chinese, and we were merely rediscovering them. His predictions made me uncomfortable, but I have gradually come to see that such a theory is never actually fulfilled in its ghastly logical extremism. The direction always develops quirks and corners in which one can enjoy oneself. Horses vanished from the streets of Dublin, but since World War II, riding has grown extraordinarily both in the Old World and the New. He was frankly pessimistic, and rather enjoyed being so, about the future of farming. Farms, I remember, were all to be huge, mechanized units run by big business. Somehow the trend he spoke of has always failed to complete itself. He did not live to see the effects of the atom bomb in the post-World War II world, but he would certainly have been the most surprised man alive to realize that the said bomb has preserved us from a world war for a longer period than ever before in modern civilization.

As far as I was concerned, my father's outlook may have been unsympathetic, but it was certainly not that of a bully. He genuinely wanted me to do what I wished to do, and not just what would make money and be the proper thing, even if he did not understand why I was interested in nothing but animals and "highbrow" books. This degree of toleration in him was certainly partly because he knew very well that he himself had never been allowed to follow his choice of a profession. That choice would certainly have been in favor of carpentry. But as I have said, his father had been District Inspector of the Royal Irish Constabulary—quite a high job in their social hierarchy, though perhaps a bit diminished because everyone knew that the top officers of this police force had been recruited exclusively from those who had failed (but just barely failed) to pass into Sandhurst, the school for British army officers. But my grandfather would have been horrified at the idea of having a son who made his living with his hands. So my father was given a reasonably good secondary education at a Dublin private school and at eighteen was shot into the Sun Insurance office, Dublin central branch. Somehow, the hope of the uncle's influence never exactly worked out, perhaps because the said uncle was apparently an alcoholic; and my father ended up in his Dublin job as accountant for the office. He had a fairly respectable salary, as middle-class salaries then went, of about four hundred a year at its best, with the company paying his income tax. He was, I am afraid, bored much of the time; anxious too on occasions such as the annual audit by the representative of a London firm. Then my father would work at the office for weeks in the evening, as well as by day, trying to discover the meaning of a discrepancy in the books of sums as tiny as ten shillings. If this discrepancy existed, it might of course hide a much larger blunder. The strain of this visibly told on him, and it would be repeated every year. All of this makes me—as I usually am not—very pleased about the existence of computers. I am really glad of the joy he had in gardening, and also glad that he took relatively early retirement and bought a plot of land in what was then the country district of Churchtown, where he built a bungalow; and for the six or seven years left them, my mother and he were, I think, extremely happy.

My mother was a more adventurous and complex character. She too had come from this dismal, shabby genteel class, just one generation away from landowners, and army and navy officers, or ladies and gentlemen living on fairly satisfactory annuities. In most of the cases that I was aware of, the decline of the members of the family seemed due to personal reasons, or just the shift of economic viability of the means at their disposal. I remember when I was about ten and usually had to spend Sunday afternoons at the aunts' house. When I was profoundly bored, one of my aunts who knew how to interest me turned over to me old "papers," long kept in the family safe. Some of these were Russian Imperial bonds, and others were share certificates in a system of street railways in Buenos Aires. These were the sort of things the generation before my aunts invested in, poor things.

My mother and her sisters had all been trained in needlework and instructed by governesses, in order that they in turn would make some sort of a living from needlework and governessing. I have always been able to enter into the feelings of Jane Fairfax in *Emma* and those of Jane Eyre. I knew and cared for my aunts and knew quite a few like them and saw the frustration and loneliness of the governess and companion kind of women, sexually starved and endlessly condemned to a kind of professional self-suppression. It is only fair to say that this destiny was especially true of my mother's sisters. My father's sisters struck out much more boldly and were among the first women in Dublin to achieve real jobs, executive and nursing jobs and the like—and near the top, too. But it was a bitterly hard struggle and demanded far too much above what it would be reasonable to expect in levels of attainment.

My mother was clever, optimistic, and of a disposition so unaffectedly cheerful that she always seemed to be able to ride out the debts, the disappointments when my father did not rise higher in the office, and the family three-week holidays at the seaside (regular holiday places like Wicklow and Arklow about thirty miles from Dublin) or at the country cousins' farms in Tipperary. These last, I am quite sure, were hardly very exciting for her. But she was capable of more day-to-day gaiety than anyone I ever knew. I have seen her charm my father out of his occasional fits of melancholy or anxiety with her infallible human touch for making him feel that ultimately everything was all right. Understanding people was her real gift, and the couple loved one another very deeply. I never had the least occasion to doubt it.

She was also a brilliant cook, which is something uncommon in Ireland, and knew how to make meals of character from quite cheap ingredients like rabbits, and fish like cod and whiting which are by nature exceedingly dull, and intestines such as tripe, and cow heel. Thanks to her, I grew up with an inherent inclination to eat any kind of food provided that it was spicy and exciting.

The last time I saw her was after I had spent some six months in Britain and the Continent. I had had a sabbatical from the university and I was on the point of making up my mind to move to Ireland for a part of every year, if I could manage to buy a farm there. I got mumps when I was at home with my parents, and my mother nursed me through them. She had had a stroke two years before and had miraculously almost completely recovered, but she was told that this might recur at any time. I think she was very glad of the opportunity to nurse me again, though my father naturally was somewhat irritated that she should have the extra work to do. I had also brought two grandchildren with me, and he felt that she had been put upon, considering her state of health. So, in some ways, it was not a very happy time, and my mother was also partly aware that my marriage was in trouble. When I came to go away, both of us were crying at the sense of the imminent final parting, made all the sharper because I would very probably be returning to Ireland so soon, if she would only last it out. We said goodbye through the tears, and I made for the door and she called me back: "We have never parted, all the times we have, in tears—and we won't do so now." We *did* in fact take some minutes, and the tears dried. I never saw her again. She had another stroke less than six months later and never recovered consciousness, and she died before I could get over from America.

Our household like most households of my boyhood, Protestant as well as Catholic, was very puritanical. Only very gradually did I make my escape from the sheer weight of Sunday church in the morning and often in the evening too, and even worse, the resolute ban on any form of public entertainment on that day. No theater, and no cinema, which was just beginning to be important. The theaters themselves were open on Sunday only on the rarest occasions, and all the regular shops were closed. There was a starkly respectable dullness about everything from morning to night. Eventually, I struck against the church bit of it. This was not really so much a resistance against religion. I loved the rhythms and the enchantment of the seventeenth-century Book of Common Prayer, which was standard in the Episcopalian church my parents went to; and of course I had been made to learn, and thoroughly enjoyed doing so, long passages in the Authorized Version. I think if I had been asked honestly by someone trustworthy, I could have answered truly that I believed in some sort of God, though it would have been hard to go beyond that—perhaps, a sense that there was some controlling force in the world that was not human. I know I strongly resisted any notion that if man possessed a soul, animals did not possess one as well. But religion in its practical manifestations repelled me as a piece of complacent stuffiness. My rebellion against going to church led to a considerable row between my father and myself, but softened through my mother's influence—I always thought she was bored by the church atmosphere herself. I was already fifteen and was let go my own way, though I am afraid my breakaway made a permanent mark on my father. I heard him refer to it, in quite bitter terms, a year before he died. From about fifteen on, they also worried about my sexual life. It was a matter of great concern that David should not meet with the "wrong" kind of girls—not without some foundation in fact. However, this worked out with all the usual halfway houses in sexual experience until I went to college at seventeen, and after that neither of my parents ever commented on my sexual behavior. All in all, as I think about my parents' treatment of me in these matters compared with, say, that of Theobald and Christina in Butler's *Way of All Flesh* (both sets of parents were ostensibly much the same sort of believing Christians), mine come out as kind and enlightened.

As I look back on my childhood, at any rate until twelve or thirteen, no one in my family influenced me as much as my Aunt May. She was something of an oddity in her day and in her ways. One of a largely celibate family on my father's side—there were four sisters and three brothers, and my father was the only one married—she very gallantly managed to win and hold jobs unusual for a woman then. After an education which stopped at fifteen, she got into an insurance office and rose to be chief clerk, then assistant manager. In 1920, when she had served the company for a number of years, the City Life Insurance Co. went bankrupt; and at thirty, Aunt May was without a job. She was already an excellent typist, but she turned herself into a legal typist, which is something much more complicated. (Incidentally, I first learned to type at age eight on Aunt May's typewriter.) She attended the Four Courts, Dublin's legal center, and took dictation from the barristers and solicitors as a freelance copyist. At this, she was an instantaneous success. Simultaneously, she secured for herself the agency for Roneo, a very early version of photocopier, and sold these machines to the lawyers by the dozens. She also became a canvasser for a big laundry which bore what was to become the ill-fated name of the Swastika. All middle-class families then sent out their laundry to be done and redelivered to the house. I never knew and still do not, at least not exactly, how Aunt May could convince so many of those with whom she came in contact of her ability to perform what they wanted. But I have some clues. She was an attractive and amusing woman and almost totally unselfconscious. She had a strong streak of the unusual in her whole personality, and that in Ireland goes further in winning popularity than in many other places. She was also persistent without being annoying. She always said, "All right, take me on. If I don't increase the sales or do better the job you want done, or bring in new territory, fire me. I won't complain." She had an almost ferocious directness and a kind of polite respect which concealed a complete want of conventional deference, all of which were very telling. I also don't know how she managed to combine such a collection of jobs: selling, typing, and all the things she did for other people or her own amusement. Later, she took some of the heat off by concentrating most of the typing into a single secretaryship for a well-known barrister, for whom she worked most evenings and had his briefs ready for him by ten the next morning. For most of her life, until late middle age, she was earning between four and eight hundred pounds a year. In those days, that was a high average even for a middle-class man.

She always liked me, partly because we shared a love for animals, and also because I loved Dickens and so did she. I still have a complete set of India-paper Dickens which Aunt May gave me, one or two at a time, and there was a whole world of private jokes between us based on a verbatim knowledge of his novels. I remember her doing a most realistic rendering of the ghastly old clothes dealer in *David Copperfield* who frightened the young David so much on his walk to Canterbury, when he had to approach him and try to sell him his jacket. The old lunatic would charge out at the boy and try to drive him away with threats and screaming "Goroo, goroo!" Aunt May was marvelous with the goroos.

She had set her heart on my going to the university, which did not look a very likely possibility considering my own family's finances. So she bought a policy with her insurance company to cover my college education. That went down the drain with the assets of the City Life. But Aunt May retrieved the situation. Her cousin Nicholas Grene of Grenepark offered her (I do not know really whether the invitation originated with her or him—he was a man of tremendous generosity and kindness for whom I had an unending admiration) to take what cash she could afford, a matter of twenty to thirty pounds, and invest it in one or two bullocks to be grazed on Grenepark. They were sold each year for a good profit, or sometimes for only slightly more pounds than they had cost, and the money all reinvested in others. After ten years, in theory (and oddly enough in fact), something like three hundred pounds would be available for David's university education. At that time, tuition fees in Trinity were only twenty-five pounds a year. As it turned out, Aunt May's and Nicholas's interest in my welfare was not put to the test. I won an entrance scholarship, then called a Sizarship, to Trinity which gave me freedom from fees for all four years and other benefits. Aunt May got her money back with the profits, and I don't know what she did with it, but certainly something good and useful. When I was fifteen to seventeen, I worked for Nicholas during all the summers and saw the cattle grazing that would be security for my education. Here again I felt the depth of my association with farming and learning, and also my gratitude toward Aunt May and Nicholas.

Aunt May also started me riding. As I lived almost all the year in Dublin, we were dependent on whatever animals were for hire. Aunt May never thought of going to a riding school, which though not as numerous as now, were there all the same. Somehow that would have been too obvious and uninteresting a solution for her. Instead, as she cycled about (for she took her bicycle to work and on business everywhere in Dublin, till she was knocked down from it by a truck and nearly killed when she was over seventy), she watched carts or gigs for the label "For hire," which was common in those times. She would instantly accost the driver and make a deal with him for horse or pony, or in early days donkey, for riding. Usually, the people were surprised, as I came to see when I appeared on the scene several days later, but they were glad enough to earn the two or three shillings an hour which hiring the animal with its vehicle would have brought in from a more conventional customer. Of course, these were hardly ideal mounts. Mostly, they were clumsy, having almost never been ridden, or they were tired or starved or in various ways unsuitable. But it was an intensely exciting process, this continual meeting with new challenges. Aunt May was abetted in all this by Sergeant Major O'Leary, ex–South Irish Horse regiment, who had been in the insurance office before World War I and returned there afterward. I can still see his queer, purplish face; he had been gassed in the war, and his eyes were still askew after it. He was Aunt May's constant friend and also a cyclist. Together, they pursued me in my amateur riding ventures around quiet Dublin streets. I had already ridden donkeys when I was a child, spending holidays in

Tipperary. But it was Aunt May (and O'Leary) who bought me my first saddle. This was a great occasion. O'Leary, after the fashion of his kind then, insisted on my riding bareback for a year (I suppose I must have been about ten when the saddle was bought) to attain a proper seat. I more than doubt the soundness of that idea, which is now largely abandoned; and I certainly remember a number of brutal falls on quiet but very hard Dublin streets, a particularly unpleasant one on Mespil Road, just off Leeson Street. But Aunt May and O'Leary always reassured me and made me feel pleasantly gallant when I remounted.

I have never been a really good rider. The circumstances of my life between Ireland and America, and between academia and farming, meant that I did not get a chance to hunt (for foxes or hares) steadily till middle age, hunting beginning in November and going on till April. When I lived in Ireland, I would have been in school for most of those periods, and when I was a young instructor in America, I did not have the kind of money needed to hunt there. However, I did get to hunting when I was over forty and went on till almost seventy, and thank God I still get around on a pony in my Irish farm, and in America on a horse of my own in the forest preserves. I have trained and driven a lot of horses mainly for work, but also for traps and buggies, and though I am not, as I said, a good rider, being basically clumsy and strong rather than patient and subtle, I have an instinctive feeling for horses and get on well with them. I have also the most intense pleasure in the association.

Aunt May was a very devout Evangelical Christian, but unlike many of that persuasion, she was no fanatic and quite without the bitterness of Puritanism. She neither smoked nor drank, but never held it against those who did both or either. I remember hearing a conversation between her and her Presbyterian minister, a man she greatly admired, when he spoke approvingly of Prohibition and the Volstead Act. She disagreed with little in the minister's opinions, but at the expression of this one she struck in, "I think many people drink and take no harm from it, and if they are to be debarred from it, I see no great merit in refusing it either." She had one very loved brother who was an alcoholic, so her moderation in temperance questions was all the more remarkable.

She showed much the same temper in most aspects of her religion. Hers was a kind of Protestantism bred of an intense conviction of a personal relation to her God, of which her prayers were the expression. Though she especially loved the Presbyterian service with its extempore prayers (which as a boy and now I find unattractive), she would go to an Episcopal church or a Catholic chapel, if on a Sunday she was somewhere where there was no service of her own variety available. About the differences in the forms of Christianity, she was strong and outspoken. I remember that she used to organize a Christmas party for very poor children in a slum district in Dublin. For this, she collected funds from her fellow parishioners in the Presbyterian parish of Adelaide Road. Aunt May had a passion for popular forms of elementary drama. Punch and Judy and circuses were meat and drink to her. The centerpiece of the children's party used to be a Punch and Judy puppet show owned by an old man who carried it around in a donkey cart. I saw it when I was about eleven and thought it marvelous. My mind still links it to the scenes with Codlin and Short in *The Old Curiosity Shop*. But the second year that Aunt May ran it she was approached by an elder of the Adelaide Road parish who, with a decent embarrassment, told her that he had been given to understand "that many of the children at the party supported by Presbyterian funds had been Roman Catholic." He hesitantly suggested that this should not be allowed. Aunt May with her usual yet always unexpected directness blew up. "Do you imagine that *poor* children in Dublin can be drawn exclusively from the Protestant population? I won't have that distinction made. If you don't give me the money, I will try to find those who will. If I fail, I will try to piece it together from money of my own. But this party is for children, Protestant, Catholic, Jewish or anything else who are too poor to have a Christmas party otherwise. That is all that matters to me about it." Of course she was as always so brutally blunt that the unfortunate rich elder retired, totally defeated. The encounter gains by knowing that the elder was owner of the large laundry of which Aunt May was the employee.

In a very simpleminded way, Aunt May tried to work out her belief in the universal and equal value of religions. She talked to me about it when I was quite young, when she took over the job of getting me to learn by heart large quantities of both Old and New Testaments. Admittedly, both of us loved the roll of the language of the Authorized Version, but Aunt May also gave me as a reward for my learning sixpence a stint, which I spent either on white mice, guinea pigs, or books. She was strong on the view that the Jews were the specially chosen of God. She stressed the Jewish birth of Christ and removed to a safe vagueness those Jews who cooperated with the Roman government in his trial. But she insisted that the Jews as such had some mystical partnership with God's revelation to men, and that it was this revelation from God which led the Jew Paul to extend Christianity to the Gentiles. Moreover, she once rather daringly said to me that she wondered if missionaries were a good idea, because God must know how to give peoples the religion which was appropriate to them. It was clear that she had no similarly certain conviction that He had enlightened the missionaries to go and convert the Africans. This was for her the extreme case, since she had probably the very vaguest notions of what Africans believed. Something "pagan" no doubt, because all "organized religions" were people who believed in God in their own way. Aunt May believed in the superiority of Christianity among modern religions, but she trusted that in the past God had a purpose in gradually revealing himself, and that in the present the Chinese, Indians, and Japanese were operating under some similar dispensation.

What I have remarked on so far makes Aunt May look like a convinced Liberal. She was, too, in a way. But the fashion in which someone of her persuasion and class grew up ironed in kinks which at least have the merit of relieving or avoiding the dull, if praiseworthy, aspects of the Liberal. Because of a very inadequate education, and I am afraid I must also add because of a passionate simplemindedness as to the dubious values of learning and cleverness, Aunt May had almost no sense of what the transmission of the basic texts of Christianity meant. The joke of the seventeenth century as to whether the serpent in Eden spoke Hebrew, or what language he spoke, covered a reality for her. She unconsciously believed that the words of the Authorized Version were the words of God and, in the New Testament, the words of Christ. Her rejection of bigotry in the matter of Catholic and Protestant was good, but it involved an utter rejection and ignorance of the nature of theology. So, at times, she was without a sense of humor, and this was for her the extremest violation of her own nature. I remember once awakening her real anger—one of the very few such times—for my enjoyment of Rupert Brooke's poem, "Heaven." She was shocked at my relish of "And under that almighty fin, the littlest fish may enter in" which as a "parody of one of the most beautiful passages of the Bible is horrid blasphemy." On the other hand, the passage that I loved equally, "And in that Heaven of all their wish, there shall be no more land, say fish," Brooke's parody of the Book of Revelation's "And there shall be no more sea," sailed right by her.

Of course as a child I had no way of evaluating Aunt May's ideas, though it is curious to note how what she said has stuck in my mind, in her very phrases. But I know Aunt May's greatest merit and her greatest power over this child's mind, at least, was that her religious ideas never left her complacent or pompous, as so much of the face of practiced religion often did. She used constantly to quote to me, "He that shall seek to save his life the same shall lose it, and he that seeks to lose his life the same shall save it," and "Judge not, that ye be not judged."

The end of the story of Aunt May—I mean the narrative of her life—was sad as all too often is the end of someone who affected many of her friends and contemporaries as a kind of figure of fun, true and good, but comical in her intensity and her isolation from the mediocrity of good sense. When she was eighty, she began to be rather funny in the head. Her banker finally called me and said that he would have to take away her check book because she was constantly giving away somewhat large sums to every stranger who appealed to her—and she really had very little money to give away. By now, her sisters and brothers were all dead, and she was living in Dublin quite alone. I used to go up from Wicklow and see her once or twice a month, but for a long time I did not find anything in her way of life which was uncommon or extraordinary, except for her banker's statement. Then one day her clergyman, a Church of Ireland man (because her old church, the Presbyterian one, was now too far for her to go to on a Sunday), told me that he had conversations with her when she seemed full of imaginary terror, and he wondered whether she should be living alone. She had several times almost burned herself and the house. I took her then to live with us on the farm in Wicklow. She had always loved the farm and for a while everything went well. But gradually things began to go wrong. She would get up at night at times and think the house was afire or would tell me that the housekeeper who worked for us was trying to poison us. As usual with Aunt May, she always made a fuss and was very loudly explicit about anything she thought. I had then two little children six and ten, and they got very frightened. I could not let this go on, but it was extremely difficult to know what to do. When these senile disturbances were over, she was perfectly clear in her head, and they were never, as far as I could see, recalled by her. I finally decided on a bold course, because I loved and admired her so. Although she was very deaf since the accident with her bicycle and the truck, she could always hear what I said to her. I told her what had happened and said honestly that I would do whatever she wanted me to. She answered at once, "If things are like that you must put me in a home. I have prayed my God that this should not happen, but not my will but His. I will sign whatever is necessary." I took her to a home, the best we could find, and she was able to pay for it with her own funds. I saw her several times thereafter—actually no more than twice or three times, because mercifully she was dead within less than two months. The people of the home liked her but felt frustrated because of her deafness. There was then no television, and she could not hear the radio. But she read the novels she loved, Dickens and Walter Scott and

Jane Austen, and of course the Bible. Except for the moments of dementia, she was, I think, fairly happy. She welcomed me when I came there with a love that made me feel totally inadequate. I saw each time that she was going downhill, and one morning the hospital called me to say that they had just found her dead. When we took her to be buried in Mount Jerome, the Protestant cemetery where her family is buried, I had engraved on her tomb, "Well done, good and faithful servant; enter into the rest of thy Lord." I meant to emphasize the personal adjective. Hers was an odd kind of Lord, but I like to think she did not trust to Him in vain.

4

Dublin (With Animals)

I grew up in a Dublin which had a more individual and distinctive character than that of today—in appearance anyhow. The
most striking elements of the visual aspect of a city, especially
a relatively old city, are the traffic, which might be described
as its face, and the buildings which border it (particularly
when the buildings and the road are close to one another) as
its soul—its historical inner being. The two interact, the traffic affecting markedly the appearance of the buildings which
you pass, depending on the length of time it takes you to pass
them. If you drive through the older parts of Dublin in a car,
it is quite impossible, even at moderate automobile speeds,
to take in the dimensions and impression of the great powerful eighteenth-century houses. You must walk, ride a bike,
or travel by carriage. Walking is perhaps the best. That is all
right for visitors, but it ends in the complete unseeingness of
the regular car passengers. Earlier, when one often drove by
in horse-drawn vehicles, there was a naturalness in how you
took in the sight of these houses. Without your noticing it,
their beauty and dignity captivated you. As things are now,
even when you are on foot, they really look like and are museum pieces for contemplation when you are quite at liberty
to look at museum pieces.

Quite the opposite is true of a modern city like Chicago; the motor traffic traveling between the vast skyscrapers on the one side and the immensity of the Lake on the other cannot dwarf either the buildings or the Lake. Furthermore, when you see the city, you see it at a considerable remove even in your car, and can take in the towering majesty of the buildings to which the only rival is the Lake, now angry with crashing waves, now with huge ice-capped crests. The cars between don't matter. They just look like little beetles. But then Chicago is not for walking, not, that is, if you want to see it. It is a modern city with face and inner being in sensible relation to one another. Motor cars and eighteenth-century buildings are not like this at all.

In the Dublin of my boyhood and youth, horse traffic predominated. All light deliveries were done by horses, and much heavy stuff like coal removal as well. Taxis did not ply in the streets of Dublin till 1926. Of course, there were private cars, but not one-third of those now there. The electric trams were still there and the canal boats with locks at the principal bridges. The whole showed a kind of careless vitality; you can still see it in photographs taken any time until the middle twenties. The last time I saw such diversity and excitement in traffic was recently in India, where in cities of the north like Jaipur and in the south like Mysore, there were oxcarts, camel carts, tongas, and the occasional elephant. This was of course much more exotic than my Dublin of old days, but it awakened in me again the recollection of how interesting it used to be to look at a street full of traffic.

Dublin now, like almost all cities, is a melee of the same surging cars, vans, trucks, the same dull noise, the same stink of oil. The only remaining difference between vehicles is in size and color; otherwise all is tin and steel. The horse vehicles were not nearly so standardized as their mechanical successors. Above all else, it was the sense of life that pervaded traffic. Live animals cannot be standardized. But the power to observe this arises only when there is variation to stimulate it. Otherwise, it disappears, and there is only a superficial notice of color or size. The older traffic was pervaded by the struggle of the living creature to use its strength in the service of the driver. The subjugation of the animal and the skill of the driver, at its best, transformed work into a continual experience, and that was communicated to those who watched— even half watched.

Perhaps the disappearance of the horse from the modern city does more than dull the distinctive aspect of traffic. Animals are the last personal contact of the modern city dweller with a world outside the city, except for pets. This seems to me a huge loss. Where every proceeding of one's ordinary life is constructed to be responsive to a skill in pushing buttons or pulling levers, one must lose at once the sense of compromise between enforced obedience and willing agency which is the essence of the horse/driver relationship. All horses have to be taught obedience, which in the beginning they are unwilling to give, by the process unpleasantly called breaking. But no intelligent user of horses would deny that there develops a partnership where the subordinate member also feels bound to the partnership for a special kind of excitement which can finally become pleasure. Of course, there always were, and still would be if the situation had continued, brutal or insensitive drivers who kept the legs of an ill-fed, ill-used animal going with the whip. They misused the horse exactly as a minimum of modern drivers misuse the engine-powered car. But these were heavily in the minority. The bread van drivers, the milk cart drivers, and the wagon drivers worked in the closest and most sensitive relation to the power that moved their vehicles in their circumstances of traffic and the special skills of their trade. And every child in every house knew and admired his particular delivery horse. It is an easy modern assumption that since some horses were ill-treated and some even cruelly treated, it is better that they should not be in the streets at all. This is an argument hard to refute if those who maintain it see no special value in the association of men and animals anyway. The animal itself can hardly be expected to have strong views on its survival as a species.

But the effect on human beings of the disappearance of the horse from cities, preceded by that of the cows, pigs, and poultry which were still part of the outlying city life in my boyhood in

Dublin, is more obvious and regrettable. The complete understanding of the use of the horse was, of course, largely confined
to cabmen and delivery van drivers. But the rest of the people
were aware of the importance of the horse in ordinary living, and
before their eyes all the time was the evidence of a chain of being
in which they and all domestic animals were linked together. As
of now, the lack of knowledge of horses as motive power, and of
the role of the domestic animals as providers of food, produces
in city men and women a special blankness of sensibility. There
are mechanical contrivances for power inexplicable in their operation. There is processed food where the kinship of the food
to the once living animal has certainly become so little visible
that it has almost vanished. There is, in fact, nothing but human
beings in the light of which to understand life directly. The result
is that, leaving horses aside for the moment, domestic animals
have become for most people a kind of bricks and mortar for
the production of necessary goods. This is also tempered by an
exaggerated attack of anthropomorphism which is delighted to
feel that the animals of which they remain aware, such as riding
horses, should certainly never work hard. It is scarcely decent to
make them work at all. But the public most emphatically does not
want to know about the brutalities of factory farming, because
they believe that this is a necessary feature of modern living.

As I have said, I have always been attracted by association
with a small community of animals. It started with my white
mice, guinea pigs, and rabbits; then with my mother's flock of
laying hens that I managed for her for a few years from the time
I was twelve. And during all my childhood, I was a devotee of the
Dublin Zoo. It was and still is, I think, nearly the perfect zoo—
small enough for a constant visitor to know all the animals, and
the zoo itself set in a not-so-tame park which is indeed a part of the
huge half-wild Phoenix Park that has been open to the public since
the eighteenth century, at the northern edge of the old limits of
Dublin. In those early days, we were allowed to feed the animals.
I know that the result was all too often to cause them digestive illness. After holidays, like Sunday, the unfortunate monkeys were

often sick for two or three days. Undoubtedly, it is better for the animals to be fed properly balanced diets devised by proper medical authorities. But one quite personal advantage for me in the old system was that, through the keepers, I got to know what the various animals like best to eat and what was good for them. So I used to bring cold boiled potatoes for the monkeys and the occasional tin of Golden Syrup (a commercial brand of molasses) for the bears. It was a special delight, I remember, to watch one very large brown bear take a look, smell the tin, and smash it with his huge paw and lick the Golden Syrup as it oozed out. I must have seemed an odd little boy, but Flood, the old keeper of the lion house, was very kind to me and would take me behind the official cages to play with his lion cubs, who shared a cage with Flood's Irish terriers during the absence of the lioness off and on during the day.

What I wanted and want from animals is to share with them a world that is theirs, not mine. I do not want to pretend that they are like me, but I want to harness a unit of that world into the world of human use and pleasure. The means must always be observation, feeding, and management. I want the animals to live their independent lives modified only by their necessary functional dependence on man. I realize that a higher form of relation to animals is that of the now many men and women who live with chimps, gorillas, or orangutans in the jungle or with wolves in Canada; mine is a much humbler version since it is practiced without the discomforts, hardships, and loneliness. Also, it deals with animals whose lifestyles have been modified by thousands of years of domestication. But the reaching out to another kind of creature, living on a continuum with ourselves physically and mentally, but significantly different in degrees—that is the same in both cases. If successful, it is to gain the ultimately foreign language, when those that speak it to you are without powers of generalizing reflection, but vivid with moment-to-moment enjoyment or pain; with passions like lust and anger, with feelings of motherhood and friendship—for friendship between animals certainly exists—in a pure form untainted by ambiguity. The reality of animals' experience is plain to view, and when nasty, fairly remediable. Certainly domestic animals belong in man's scheme of things because of their usefulness to him. There can be no doubt of that, and such unqualified and inevitable submission of the animals makes it illogical to talk of animals' rights, as people often use the phrase nowadays.

But this does not do away with human duties to the animals. That is, to give creatures whose wants are very similar to our own, space adequate to move about in, and to keep them in such a way that their relationships to one another are more or less those of normal animal life. Hens with a cage space of a few inches, pigs packed into overheated pens devoid of any object of interest, are being tortured and quite unjustifiably. The signs of their neuroses are plain. The hens tear one another's feathers until with a satanic mercy their owners have them debeaked. The pigs chew one another's tails off, and now nearly all fattening pigs have their tails removed when a few days old for fear that these later wounds will cause death or infection. Pigs suffer especially under these conditions because they are by nature intensely curious and bent on discovering things. Give ten of them a pen with a bare concrete floor, without bedding (which saves cleaning) and grain thrown naked on the floor and water in automatic troughs, with only aimless movements to form a self-generated routine, and of course they go mad. I know a farm where sows stand each in a pen too narrow for her to turn round in. They can stand up or lie down—that is all. They never come out until they are about to farrow and then they are moved to another pen surrounded by an iron farrow crate designed to prevent the mother accidentally lying on the little pigs or perversely murdering them, as in her unnatural misery she sometimes does. Thank God some resentment of these conditions is beginning to percolate through society, and in both Europe and the United States there are now some legal limits on the restrictions of space for poultry and pigs. It remains to be seen what form of enforcement of these measures can be possible without an army of snoopers.

The only effective remedy would be a change in society's attitude toward the torture, and that would involve really understanding something about the animals, instead of the enjoyment of empty sentiment. The general public is acutely aware of cruelty to pets such as dogs and cats and cage birds, but any increase in the price of eggs due to free range for the fowl is bitterly resented.

Horses in modern society have indeed attained a peculiar status. Over much of the earth, they are no longer used for ordinary purposes of animal power, as they were for several thousand years. But from the beginning of the horses' domestication, they were not only used for power in the ordinary fashion. They were for speed, excitement, beauty, luxury—the glory of the rich man's luxury, Aeschylus calls them in the *Prometheus Bound*. This original feeling has survived, and today has extended its scope. By far, most of today's horse users are people of quite modest means; and although racing and show jumping are very popular as entertainment in television and otherwise, there is a much greater number of riders who are using rough, undeveloped land, unsuitable for agriculture, for pony trekking in Europe, and trails in forest preserves in the States. It is interesting to note that there is no difficulty at all in making horse owners of this modern sort aware of their duties to their horses. Indeed, their view of the animals is not merely sentimental; it is shamelessly anthropomorphic. But few people feel at all like that about cattle, sheep, pigs, or poultry. They think that such animals are much less sensitive than the horse. So they are, to some extent. But the sensitivity of the ridden horse is entirely limited to half-enforced and half-willing subjection to man's purposes expressed by hands, legs, leather gear, and whip. It is from this combination that the peculiar quality, the other half of the centaur, magically develops. His younger owners do not realize that there was very largely the same sensitivity and satisfaction in the horses of yesterday who pulled carriages and carts and powered every operation on the farm. Those older breeds of horses were more often misused or mistreated, but not habitually nor indeed very frequently.

What does my memory emphasize most of the Dublin buildings that I knew as a child and a schoolboy? The most beautiful and striking parts of Dublin are all within the space of about a mile or two. They are almost all directly or indirectly creations of the late eighteenth and early nineteenth centuries. Those great squares of parkland surrounded by dwelling houses four stories high with their absolutely plain fronts, high, narrow windows, and air of dignified gravity: that is Merrion Square and Fitzwilliam Square. When I knew them first, they were lived in by doctors and lawyers. Then for a while they were divided into flats, but even these were very expensive both to rent and to keep up. They had been built as grand town houses by the aristocracy of the 1780s and 1790s, and everything like roofs and staircases needed constant attention and care. Now they are mostly government offices and such. The insides of the houses have been almost entirely altered to allow central heating and overcome woodworm. But the fronts remain, and frame big open uncluttered streets. For concentrated effect, I have seen almost nothing like them in any city I have visited.

The grander, or simply larger, versions of roughly the same age are the Bank of Ireland (once the seat of Ireland's parliament before the Act of Union,) a vast, overpowering building directly opposite the front of Trinity College, which itself dates from Georgian times. To my mind, it is only these two structures which by sheer size and beauty manage to dominate the immensely confused and intricate motor traffic that swirls round them. It is startling to look at old pictures of that part of Dublin painted in the early nineteenth century. Then the two buildings look relatively lonely, for even the horse traffic of those days makes no impression of the crowding of today, and so the sense of power and domination of the buildings is conspicuously less. But it is still exciting to be able to walk about in this magnificent part of Dublin. Those buildings were the relics of the British administration, and there have been times within the last seventy years that small-mindedness and hatred threatened to fail to keep them safe from the inroads of development and road-building. Such hostility together with greed did destroy significant parts of Stephen's Green, and the battle is by no means over yet. But enough feeling has been aroused so that I doubt if either the lunatic nationalism which blew up Nelson's Pillar, or the sheer philistine greed that permitted the bulldozing of the most complete remains of early Danish Dublin to build the particularly ugly Dublin City Council

Headquarters, will go much further. Very slowly, even the embedded anger of the folk memories of actual oppression, and even worse the separation of the two political parties which arose from the Civil War of 1921 to 1923, are beginning to break down before the realization that what we have in Ireland is a nation of hugely disparate elements—Celts, Danes, Anglo-Norman, British, and that peculiar breed of the past, the Anglo-Irish Ascendancy— and that the important matter is to see the whole as a united Irish nation, to some degree a genuinely new Ireland. I think also Ireland's participation in the European Community has done a lot for a country which always seems to have wanted a degree of small, self-conscious identity in the middle of a bigger and more varied unit of opportunity. There was a time when that was satisfied by the British connection, especially from 1830 on. Access to the army for everyone, lower and upper class alike, and for the upper class the British Civil Service for the running of the Empire, did serve this purpose. Then there was the big emigration to America and latterly to Australia, but in both cases the emigrants became citizens of a new country, and there remained of their Irishness only some sentimental feelings. In a new Europe, there may be able to coexist a special association between Ireland and the nations of the Continent. If that happens, the remnants of the nationalism which has been such a stumbling block since 1920 will be, one hopes, as dead as the dodo.

Then there is the River Liffey, running through the heart of the city, and between its banks marking the barrier of the old Dublin as it existed from the eighth century till the sixteenth when the inhabitants began to grow more numerous, and Dublin stretched out south and north. It is a wonderfully suggestive river, even dirty and polluted as it tends to be now. If the truth be known, it probably was polluted during a great deal of its history, since it served as a sewer for the city for hundreds of years. But a mysterious river it is, especially in the early misty mornings of summer. I remember very well that for weeks before my final exams in Trinity when I could not sleep, I would walk along the quays, and it always comforted me, although its suggestions of comfort were to be only vaguely understood. There is not a great deal of water traffic there nowadays—and that is also a very old problem, for the Liffey has always been somewhat too shallow for bigger boats coming in from the Irish Sea and carrying goods from Britain. I remember as a boy, though, going to the very mouth of the river near the North Wall to see the huge four-masted sailing ships carrying wheat from Australia. This went on till, if I recollect correctly, about 1927. Much of the other water traffic was in coal from Wales, since Ireland has almost no coal mines. These coal boats would also have to stop at the North Wall or thereabouts and transship the coal in great craneloads dumped onto open, flat, four-wheeled wagons. I always loved to watch and admire the patient, unmoving horses as the coal fell with a crash onto the wagons, and they would quietly, with almost no stimulus from the driver other than a shout, wheel across the road to the coalyard where the stuff was bagged and distributed through the city and the country. Between the Liffey and the two great canals, Dublin was a city where one did not easily forget the role of water in transportation. As I walked to school, I used to pass either Leeson Street Bridge or Charlemont Street Bridge, which marked locks in the canal. The canal boats in those days were towed by horses from the bank, and these would then be unhitched and led across the road while the canal boat, mostly carrying turf for burning in our small open fireplaces, was gradually raised at the locks. In or about the thirties, the Irish authorities discarded this canal boat business and let the locks and the surface of the canal degenerate—unlike both the Dutch and the British. In more recent times, the renovation has started. It looks as though there will be a profitable tourist attraction in motorized barges taking people through the Dublin canals to the rivers of Ireland.

5

The Theater

Until the age of eleven, my only experience of the theater was at the yearly Christmas pantomime, to which our whole family always went. These are not pantomimes in the strict sense of dumb show, but a traditional form of comic entertainment put on at Christmastime. The greatest of them in my time was the one done year after year at the Gaiety under the leadership of Jimmy O'Dea and Maureen Potter. These were a wonderful pair of genuinely amusing comedians, and they ran the show to suit themselves. But prior to them, it was not like that. Most of the theaters in Dublin (the Gaiety, Royal, Queen's, and Olympia) put on a separate pantomime every year. Each pantomime was sketchily based on a folk story—Cinderella, Jack and the Beanstalk, Dick Whittington, or others—and there was an intermittent effort to include a few scenes from the original story, especially the finale. All the rest of the show was given up to variety turns such as jugglers, clowns, and animal acts. One curious feature that even then stood out for me was that the hero and heroine were, conventionally, always represented by women. Thus, the principal boy was invariably a girl. I suppose this was for fear that simple sexual relations would creep across the footlights and disturb or corrupt the young. Also in a pantomime such as Cinderella, the two ugly sisters were both played by men. The men's voices, and even on rare occasions somewhat risqué jokes, enclosed an area of a cruder humorous mood suitable to its masculine representation and unthinkable for the delicacy of the women.

Every pantomime was dominated by its particular song, and depending on how catchy it was or how funny, we would hear everyone from businessmen and women to delivery boys whistling and singing it for months. I remember one of them which went like this:

> How can a guinea pig wag his tail
> If he hasn't got a tail to wag?
> All the other animals, you will find,
> Have got a little tail to wag behind.
> If they'd only put a tail on the guinea pig
> And finish up a decent job,
> Then the price of a guinea pig would go right up
> From a guinea up to thirty bob.

I am afraid that much of the funniness of this depends on knowing that a guinea is twenty-one shillings; as a coin of the realm, it had vanished even when I was a boy. But it was the unit in which you purchased various high-grade goods, such as fancy suits. I am glad to notice that it survives in similar snobbish settings. Christie's in London continued with it until the pound went metric, and you still buy racehorses in guineas in Newmarket. A shilling—twenty to the pound—was vulgarly a bob. I still know the tune of that song.

But in 1924, I had a quite different and first-time theatrical experience. Sybil Thorndike came to Dublin to play in George Bernard Shaw's *Saint Joan*. I do not know whether this preceded her London performance or was shortly afterward. In those days, Dublin was often used for a tryout by big London companies. I had had a lot of training in this particular play, because our English master in my first school had made us learn by heart many of St. Joan's speeches. He was himself a very strong lover of Shaw. However, nothing prepared me for the shock of this great performance. I had so far seen no plays proper at all (only pantomimes) and, in the cinema, the single picture *The Hunchback of Notre Dame* with Lon Chaney. I do not know how much reliable knowledge I can still retain of a performance more than sixty years ago. All the probabilities are against it. But I do know accurately some of the excitement and even fear I felt, and I dare to hope, faintly, that I remember accurately some of the voice and gestures which triggered those emotions. Very shortly thereafter, I was taken to see *Othello,* as rendered by Charles Doran. He was an actor who toured Ireland every year with his Shakespearean company. A few years after, the company was much strengthened by the addition of Anew McMaster, a brilliant player whom I saw ten years later in the same role. But even in Doran's performance as the Moor, I vividly remember my intense reaction to his "Put out the light, and then put out the light" speech. I still cannot see this play without terror, and I am quite certain that the terror has elements of the feeling of that performance all those years ago.*

It was a very exciting time to see Dublin theater, the twenties and thirties. The Abbey was again convulsed by nationalist agitation when Sean O'Casey's *The Plough and Stars* met with a reception in 1926 as hot as that which had attended the first performance of J. M. Synge's *The Playboy of the Western World* in 1907. During that performance of the *Plough,* the crowd tried to pour onto the stage and burn the curtain because the national flag, the Tricolor, was brought inside a pub by three Irish volunteers in the 1916 rising, and there was a prostitute in the bar who tried to pick up some of the guests and eventually made it with the glorious Fluther Good. I was at another performance of the *Plough* in 1932, and there were still interruptions from the audience. The Abbey audience was until quite lately most volatile, and its prejudices, national, puritan, or otherwise, were very often to the

*David Grene did a very powerful reading of that scene himself, which was recorded. See p. 165.

fore and caused both actors and directors speculative misgivings about forthcoming productions. Humor is very consistently attributed to the Irish as a people, and perhaps on the whole justly, but they certainly have shown blind spots in this regard. Would anyone really have expected that a pub would be regarded as a sordid background for the national flag? Or that the mere presence of a prostitute in that pub contaminated the enthusiasm of the volunteers? Yet that was exactly what the nationalist and the pious interrupters claimed afterward when they published their grounds for the attack.

The Abbey company was very tightly knit; such repertory companies nowadays are very rare indeed. The play changed sometimes every week, almost certainly every fortnight. To see the same actors playing widely different roles so often makes one understand the versatility of which the profession is capable. Through this, it is possible to see the extraordinary blend of artificiality and realism that underlies most theatrical creations of the Western world. To me, this early experience of the Abbey has been beyond price. I have seen quite a few productions in London over the years, many of them of Shakespeare and many excellent. And in the year I spent in Vienna, I saw some great work done by Basserman and the Thimigs, but I never again have had the opportunity of seeing great repertory covering such a number of different kinds of plays over eight years. There was also something magnetic for me about the old Abbey, besides the acting. From the time I was sixteen till I left Dublin semipermanently in 1938, I used to haunt their first nights. Always, as the bell for the rising of the curtain rang, there would be a murmur among the audience, "There is Mr. Yeats," and the poet would come down the few steps to his place in the front row, head a little bent, slightly groping myopically for his seat. I loved the early Yeats plays and poems, and as much of the middle poems as were then written and I understood. The best, in my opinion, were still to come. But he was already, I was sure, as great as the greatest lyric poets in English, and there he was alive and palpable before me. I also have seen, at a respectful distance, Lady Gregory and

Sean O'Casey. My reading world, till then shared with so very few people, was coming alive and totally realizable. In my first year in college before I had rooms there, I would walk from home to Trinity and I always went down Stephen's Green in the hope of seeing Yeats, walking along muttering from his house toward the Green itself. I was often rewarded by the sight of him.

Another freakish bit of luck—in 1929 I believe it was—a special Sunday evening performance was given at the Abbey by an English company. It was Ibsen's *Ghosts*, and the lead was played by Mrs. Patrick Campbell. I do not know how old she was then, but very near her end. She occasionally went up in her lines, and I saw her from what we called the Gods, which was the gallery of the old theater (burnt down in 1951), but it was for me an amazing thrill to see Mrs. Campbell, Shaw's greatest actress. Again, I believe that I remember some of her characteristic playing. Certainly, something from that performance hovers in my mind in all the versions of the play I have seen since.

There was something else peculiar to the atmosphere of the old Abbey. The girls at the box office, the men who moved the props, the electricians, the carpenters were blended, it seemed to me, in one working family. I have never seen any other theater quite like that. These people were all heart and soul in the venture themselves and knew all the rest of the company as friends and intimates. The other great Dublin theater then was new— the Gate, housed in a section of the beautiful eighteenth-century Rotunda. They did continental and modern plays, rather explicitly contrasting with the Abbey, which mostly dealt in Irish plays, ancient and modern, and occasionally, when they had briefly an English director if some of the regular company were in America, Shakespeare Between these two repertory companies—for the Gate was also repertory—and their very large number of plays English and foreign from the last three centuries, I do not think I could have had a better chance for developing an appreciation of drama.

6

Tipperary

In my later boyhood days, from 1927 to 1930, my secondary life—that in Tipperary—became very important to me. As long as I can remember, which means from about 1920, the family had very often spent some or all of my father's three-week holiday in summer either at Cappamurra or Grenepark, each presided over by one of the Grene brothers stemming from the Catholic branch of "cousins." I was of course part of this annual rurification in childhood. I can remember scenes in either place from the time when, at ten, I saw my first threshing of wheat and barley by the steam-powered thresher. Again, in those years Michael Morissey, the herd at Grenepark, took me round with him on all his daily surveys of cattle and sheep counting and observing, and I got my first experience of the diseases they suffer from. Also in Cappamurra I got my first experience of the dramatic death of an animal, a big bullock shot because of a broken leg. It was also in Tipperary in my early years that I learned personally the driving of horses in carts and of that enigmatic animal, the jennet, a product of a donkey mother and pony father. There was in those days nearly always a jennet in either big or small farms. In both, the jennet, he or she—both male and female were sexually active but 99 percent infertile—was used for all sorts of light jobs: carrying milk to the creamery, fetching farm supplies from railway stores, and at times used in the trap, or buggy in American terms. Jennets could do more work on less food than the pony, and at times even more than a small horse. But they had uniformly vile dispositions, with a real inclination to bite and kick human beings if the opportunity offered. Thus, for the ten-year-old, a chance to drive one of these was a real challenge; it took courage and expertise, especially when one was first inducted into the difficulties of fetching the animal from the stall and harnessing it oneself. (Ireland had, and has, almost no specimens of the other hybrid cross—a draft mare and a Spanish jackass, which produced all the great mules in America.) These childhood scenes burned into my consciousness and I can remember the details vividly still.

But it was the years 1927 to 1929 that climaxed the details in a very particular way. In 1927 Nicholas, he of Grenepark, wrote my parents. Of late they had tended to take their holidays by the seaside or go to the Continent. In the letter he said that if David was coming down in any case he would be very grateful if I could come as early as possible. His herdsman had left him; he was himself overwhelmed with work and would be glad of extra help. He didn't stress what our family already knew, that he had lost money very seriously since the end of World War I, as indeed most farmers had, but he had also been tempted into owning race-horses and lost exceedingly badly on them. Affairs were going to get worse in Irish farming through the early thirties before the war; after that the new opportunities in Europe opened up. But these were to exceed the term of his life. I was not only delighted but very proud to be asked for as someone useful, and stepped off the train at familiar Goulds' Cross with a new feeling of coming to my second home. Yes, there was Nicholas to meet me with the trap and Matchbox, his part-Hackney cob. (Grenepark's motor car had been commandeered during the Civil War in 1922, and when recovered was ruined. Nicholas never replaced it with another.) But I was taken aback when I saw Nicholas himself. There he was with his big red head and his customary red face with a welcoming smile. But he had always worn a regular suit with a gold watch in his waistcoat and carried a gold-topped cane. Quite naturally, since his work in Grenepark was entirely supervisory, seeing that the farmhands did the labor. He now wore overalls, overalls which I had then very rarely seen anywhere in Ireland, since workmen at that time used their run-down suits and once-good clothes as work uniforms. As he saw me wonder, he laughed with that unique laugh of his and said, "I have a suit for you too at home. You're really going to work, my boy." We were going to work. He had bought a milking machine, the first in Tipperary and one of the first twenty or thirty in Ireland, I believe, and was milking over forty cows. That is to say, we were going to milk the forty cows, and the man who had hitherto helped him was relieved for work with the other men in the fields. Besides this, we were fattening fifty pigs; and the care of the eighty dry, fattening cattle and two hundred sheep, which had been Morissey's job till he quit, would now have to be done by the two of us, Nicholas and myself. The eldest boy of the family, some years older than I was, was at school in Scotland. A very few years later he decided to become a novice and so only occasionally visited home. There were two more boys, of seven and three, respectively. Four girls were all at school, the eldest about sixteen and the others from six to fourteen. So nothing much was to be expected from all of these in the way of help.

I doubt if I have ever worked as hard since, as I did that summer. I had to be up about five to gather and bring in the cows. Then Nicholas and I milked them and fed the pigs from six to nine. Then there was breakfast, and after breakfast I went on the rounds of cattle and sheep. If there was anything wrong with these, I got Nicholas to come, and between us we brought the affected animals in; if they were sheep, it had also to be the herd to which they belonged. Up in the yard we could catch the particular sheep, lame or otherwise in trouble, in pens or houses. Then lunch, then a short rest or reading, and then the evening chores again. What made it harder was that Nicholas was an inveterate late-to-bedder. After eight at night he would walk with me up and down Grenepark avenue talking about livestock or himself or the way life was. He was rather a lonely man and we had always liked one another, and so I rarely got to bed before eleven-thirty—and I had to be up by five. I am inclined to think that I have also never enjoyed myself so much as in those years and those months.

Though Nicholas was good-humored by nature and even merry, he had a truly terrible temper. But even then I noticed, that though he abused his men vehemently for faults, few of them really seemed to me to heed him. At first I thought that they just dared not answer him back, but then I saw a clue to their behavior which was confirmed in my later years. His top man in those later days, the successor to Morissey, had a long talk with me the first year I was back after World War II, when Nicholas had been dead already ten years. He said, "The old master was a fright for abuse. I think he was the most frightening man when he was angry that I ever saw in my life, but Lord love you, he would fire a man with every expression of fury, but I never knew anyone to go away. He always seemed not to notice the next day that the man was still there. Now the new master—they would worry about him all right. And I suppose that's a better way to run the place." I wonder.

I remember two events bearing on this awful temper of his and his inward self-examination. Rather, the first of them shows less temper than bafflement and despair. One evening in 1929 after we had finished supper and Nicholas was standing in the machine shed talking with me, we saw a man coming up the short back avenue. He asked Nicholas if he had a job.

(That spring there were twenty men employed in Grenepark; the farm was and is over four hundred acres, and very little mechanization was then to be had and almost no system of contracting. Today I doubt if it needs more than five or six men to run it. The laborers in 1929 had, for years, earned twenty-five shillings a week—one pound five. The tram drivers in Dublin made two pounds, but the country workers usually got grass for a cow as well, and they sold a lot of eggs and chickens from their own households. Nicholas decided that, at the rate he was paying, the place would go bankrupt. So he did a most unusual thing then; he called the men together, explained the situation, and told them that if they could all take ten shillings he'd be very glad to keep them. The alternative was to reduce the total staff to ten men at a pound a week. They were to decide. They unanimously decided to take the cut and stay.)

So naturally Nicholas told the fellow in no uncertain terms that he had no work for him. The man said earnestly, "Sir, I lost my job two weeks ago. I live in Ballach (a village two miles from Grenepark) and for the last three days I have walked to every farm within ten miles of here and got nothing to do. I am in dread to go home to my wife and the children tonight and to have to tell her I still have nothing." Nicholas said nothing for a while and then he asked where exactly he had worked and how long. He answered, "Ten years." Finally Nicholas said, "Come over tomorrow morning and I'll see what I can do. But don't expect anything more than a week's work, if I can even give that much." The man turned away and I could see his face working, but he only said, "I am every way grateful, sir." When he had gone, I, a brash and unfeeling boy—I knew far more than I ought to have about the farm's finances—said to Nicholas, "Why did you do that? You know we have too many men already." He looked very thoughtfully at me and without a second's hesitation said, "David, that man is hungry. I could see it in his face. If I turned him away I could be no Christian. I couldn't even be a man in my own eyes." Need I say that the man died in Grenepark service thirteen years later, just months before Nicholas's own death?

The second story illustrates even more fully how wild the relation could be in those early days between master and man. (These were then far more meaningful terms than employer and employee.) It also shows decisively the balance in Nicholas between his willful passionateness and his latent sense of kindness and fairness. I was part of a three-way discussion on another evening similar to the first. The other man in this case was a small farmer called Tom Maloney. He was a great hero in my young eyes, for he had been a laborer sometimes in Grenepark, had bought twenty acres of his own, reclaimed another fifteen acres of bogland, and moreover was openly very fond of his wife, a rather unusual occurrence in that setting. Even then it was my dream to do something more or less as he had done; to move from whatever else there was to become an owner and a farmer. Necessarily it would be a small farm and not something like Grenepark, for although I enjoyed working with Nicholas, I had always a very strong preference for a small, one-man farm. On the evening of the discussion Maloney had come to Grenepark to talk to Nicholas about a horse he had bought and was training. Nicholas clearly liked him very much. He said, "Tom, if the new horse isn't just now up to all the work, you can borrow one of mine if you give me word ahead as to when you want him." Tom said, "You're always a generous man, sir," and turning to me, he said, "Did the master ever tell you how he chased me out of here with a gun and would have shot me? I had borrowed a mower off him and something went wrong with the damn thing and I brought it back here on a cart to show him. The master took it and looked at it and he started to curse me, and shouting all the time ran into that shed there and came out, so help me God, with a gun. I ran down the avenue as fast I could and left my cart with the mower sitting in it." Nicholas roared with laughter and without the slightest embarrassment said, "You divil, you had broken up the mower altogether. The way you do with those gorilla hands of yours with any modern machine."

I confess I am very glad Tom ran, because I wouldn't be quite certain that in his fury Nicholas wouldn't have used the gun at that moment.

In all sorts of ways Nicholas stepped into a relationship with me that was, I am half ashamed to say, vacant. He became a sort of replacement father. Many years later when I still had my first farm—the one in Lemont, Illinois—just a couple of years after the Second World War ended, I brought both my parents over to live a summer with me on that farm. My father, who was already almost seventy, started to work on building a machine shed for me and fixing up the various things that needed repair in the barn. I never had, nor have ever since had, much money on any of the three farms I have owned for what are optimistically called "improvements." But my father was very enterprising. He found all sorts of bits of timber or old metal from disused machines and indeed did wonderful things with them. After a while I began to think he could find material lying about for nearly anything I needed. He told me that he felt like the Israelites working for Pharaoh; first they had mud, etc., for the bricks and finally absolutely nothing, but the bricks still had to be made. At that time I not only loved him more naturally than I ever had, but I also had an association with him there that was vibrant and vital. It had never been quite like that in Belmont Avenue, although I certainly knew then how generous and self-sacrificing he was in the way of paying for my education; I also did value his tolerance of my "animals of all sorts" in his toolshed.

But recollections of Nicholas are full of romantic depth and mystery. In the first year I worked for him we still went to fairs— the sales which are now auction marts—with the horse and trap. Tipperary and Clonmel, the chief sites of such fairs, were ten to twelve miles off, and people began selling animals any time after 7:00 a.m. The cattle and sheep which we were selling from Grenepark had begun their walk to those towns before midnight of the previous day. We would be up by four or five the next morning and the boy in the yard would bring round the trap with lighted lanterns on it to the front door well before six. We would have eaten a sandwich or two and drunk a cup of tea in the drawing room and were then ready to start. I loved, passionately, driving along the dark roads behind the horse, the grass and trees at the sides only slightly illuminated by the trap's lamps. Toward seven we could put them out and see the morning break, as often as not, with a vivid red sky. We talked about a lot of things, inevitably very often of horses. Nicholas confided to me that his father had thought very little of him, and told him so, because he was no rider nor did he hunt with hounds. In all those years from the time his father died he had not forgotten his sense of unhappiness at the censure. It did seem to me a strange thing, though I have seen it happen a number of times since then: Nicholas loved owning racehorses and loved seeing them race, but otherwise he had never worked horses in the fields and merely drove whatever pony he had for the trap.

Nicholas also taught me other basics of farming. He would walk with me through a herd of cattle and say, "David, what weight is that bullock?" Surprisingly some farmers and even some dealers are still not much good at guessing weights. I found out very quickly that what one learns to do is to take in a number of details only half-consciously: for instance the size and prominence of shoulders and foreparts, often balanced against the undesirable lightness of the hindquarters, which is where the best cuts come from in fattening cattle. In my own case, and this maybe an accident of my American marketing experiences later, nowadays when I correctly judge the weight of an animal I see in my mind a kind of scale with the hand going round to 750, to 780, to 800, to 825 pounds and then a quiver and only a pound or two more. And with very minor differences that's what the weight is. I thought this was unique—I mean what I saw—till I found out a neighbor of mine who farmed in America near me had an exactly similar experience. That's why I imagine seeing animals weighed on a scale at markets must somehow become the language which is expressive of the observed details in structure of the animal, which one cannot in fact put together in any other way.

7

Schools

The necessities which drove me from my very early years were my enthusiasm for reading and for farming. In particular, reading Greek and Latin literature, and taking what chances of farming as my distant relationship with my Tipperary cousins afforded. But these twin loves of my boyhood divorced me very completely from the setting and interests of my parents. When they began to discover the odd sort of cuckoo* they had raised, they did everything they could to let me go the way I wanted, as far as schooling anyway; the other wishes I had were quite out of their power to gratify. In this matter of education they frequently disregarded their very limited means. I did know this, I was deeply grateful to them, and I loved them truly. But all the same a social and aesthetic snobbery became the innerspring of my being as I set out on my path. My parents sent me to a small and dubiously exclusive school (where Dicky Wood taught me) because they did not feel right about exposing me to the regular "national" schools, which were free. In a way they were right; decently,

---

*Most species of cuckoo lay their eggs in the nests of other non-cuckoo birds, for these to hatch and raise their young. So the young cuckoos are always changelings, not resembling their deceived adoptive parents.

generously right. The national schools, especially the Catholic ones, were brutally managed, as a whole, with beatings and compulsion the sole means of getting anything done. These national (state) schools were sharply divided between Protestant and Catholic, the former controlled by the Protestant clergyman of the district, and the Catholic by the parish priest. This is still the case, but in most other ways the state school system has been greatly changed and improved. After formation of the new nationalist state in 1921–22, both religious schools were very fairly and indeed generously supported by balanced payments from the government. Boys and girls, separately of course, went to these schools till about the age of thirteen, when free education ended. But in addition to this state education, there were a variety of private, also religious-run schools for those who did not want their children to mix with anyone and everyone. Simon Dedalus in James Joyce's *Portrait of the Artist* speaks of sending his son Stephen someplace where he would not be thrown in with Paddy Stink and Mickey Mud. In the state schools, from ages eight to twelve, children were taught mostly just reading, writing and sums, and it must be confessed that the people over forty in Ireland, especially the women, have a high standard of literacy. The private schools took on many of their pupils at eight, as they did me, and in theory carried us all the way till sixteen, when some of us went into banks or business houses, and the rest a year or two later went to University.

The school my parents chose for me was St. Stephen's Green and was essentially one of these small private Protestant schools. It was not a boarding school, but otherwise the atmosphere was very like that described by George Orwell in *Such, Such Were the Joys*. The fees in the bigger private schools like High School or St. Andrew's (where I went toward the end of my schooldays) were certainly rather less than in a place like St. Stephen's Green, and both varieties cost far more than what my parents should have sensibly entertained as possible for them. I believe that the smaller schools were associated with a more explicit version of gentlemanliness. In the larger private schools quite a few of the pupils came from what was very nearly working class. Anyway, my parents decided that the small and exclusive Stephen's Green was absolutely best for me, and by scraping and saving they sent me to it.

So during my schooldays—from about eight to seventeen (kindergarten occupied the years from six to eight)—I attended two Dublin private schools. I was in Stephen's Green for about seven years and St. Andrew's for two—the years directly before entrance to Trinity College. I certainly learned a great deal of languages in St. Andrew's and was well taught. But I still do not think that much which formed my mind or my intellectual interests would have happened but for one master in the first school, Dicky Wood. I can still see him, old (though not quite so old as I am now) with a red, round face and one slightly crossed eye, wearing very respectable grey suits. He had been retired from a provincial school, bigger than ours, some years before, and when he came to Dublin had been taken on as a cheap staff member at Stephen's Green. He was so excessively tenderhearted and so irresolute that he found it very hard to keep order in his class. When the boys made a row, or were talking and inattentive, he was quick to put the offenders' names in the Detention Book, but almost always succumbed to their pleas before the end of his hour and rubbed the names out again. But give him a small number of impressionable boys, and he was a different being—and his passion was for Greek literature.

I remember he started us out on a book of elementary Greek readings which featured passages in genuine ancient Greek authors, a little modified and reduced in difficulty. I should not even say "started," for he began conscientiously with the grammar, and we declined the declensions and recited the conjugations in a sort of chant. But this lasted something less than two months, and we were then confronted with the book of readings. The grammar was still drilled into us coordinately with the readings to make sure that we did not forget it. This was an entirely different way of instruction from what I had had in Latin, where the teachers kept us writing "sentences" in Latin, examined strictly for grammar and nothing else, for nearly two years before reading anything in the original language. I have no doubt about the superiority of the Dicky Wood system over my Latin learning. I suppose I am about as competent in the one language as the other now, but from those beginning years my instinctive response to the drift of the Greek periods and their meaning was much better than my rather wooden translation of the Latin. Dicky also started us reading the New Testament in Greek. We all knew lots of the English New Testament (Authorized Version) by heart, and we were absurdly proud of our ability to read the opening verses of St. John's Gospel in Greek, with a not quite mistaken belief that we understood it miraculously clearly, and as we had never known it before.

In the second year Dicky had us read the *Alcestis* of Euripides. (There were five of us in Greek; the others in our regular class, the Fourth, had chosen one of the two alternatives to Greek: German or drawing.) We were all made to take parts and read the lines dramatically, first in Greek and then in English; Dicky himself insisted on playing Alcestis. Our classroom for Greek was an unoccupied room in the huge old eighteenth-century house on St. Stephen's Green (now demolished), unswept and usually unheated. I remember Dicky dying magnificently as Alcestis, flopping very naturally on the dusty floor, declaiming her dying speech. He knew Browning exceedingly well, and Browning's version of *Alcestis* nearly by heart. It was Browning he usually recited when he came to give us the English version. We, of course, stumbled through with whatever simple translation we could manage. The bracketing of the strangely attractive and secret Greek with the excitement of the comprehensible and elegant Browning transported us—and we also in an elementary way were penetrated by what we were doing in our clumsy efforts to render the Greek.

At this point Dicky also used to teach us English literature. He discussed all of his favorite books with his pupils, and especially with me when I would walk part of the way home with him along Leeson Street. He had vivid and often unusual preferences in fiction. For instance, he was a great devotee of Walter Scott, and surprisingly both he and I chose *The Antiquary* before the others. After that I listed *The Heart of Midlothian*, and he *Old Mortality*. He was always deep in nineteenth-century novels; I hardly ever heard him speak of Fielding or Smollett or Sterne—I suppose because in those twisted Puritanical days they would have been looked upon as undesirably coarse for the young. He knew and loved Dickens and Thackeray, and especially Jane Austen and Charlotte Brontë, and was strong on the connections of Charlotte's parson father with his stories of Ireland and, in particular, between those stories and Emily's *Wuthering Heights*. He passionately loved nineteenth-century poetry, especially Browning and Tennyson, but he stopped short of modernity in Yeats. One must remember that in the mid-1920s Yeats had not yet written what seem to me his greatest poems. I also remember once being brought up short by Dicky over a disagreement with me. I was about eleven years old and given to pretending to understand what I did not. In 1924 I saw *Saint Joan* and afterward *Othello*. I ventured to say how both had moved me and how extraordinary the experience of *Othello* had been. Dicky said, rather hesitantly, "Don't you think it is a somewhat sordid story?"

I find it surprising, looking back, that even with Dicky's interest and influence as strong as it was in both classical and modern literature, I stuck resolutely to Greek rather than English as my area of concentration; for within a couple of years, from thirteen to fifteen, those of us who expected to go on to university were already setting ourselves up to specialize in those subjects that suited us best. (This very early specialization has been, and still is, one of the major differences between the English and the American systems of education.) After all, English was my native language; Greek and Latin I knew only imperfectly. Even the fragments of the two languages I had mastered were hard won and doubtfully grasped. The appreciation of literature in its elementary form, the passionate response to story or rhythm, with half-understood glimpses of "meaning" conveyed in them, were only partially present in my head in two foreign languages that were no longer evolving or in use and, therefore, in some sense dead. Yet I think my choice, if one could call such a slight inclination a choice, was not wrong. There is something in the process of learning Greek and Latin which baffles an immediate comprehension, which slows the response but does not finally diminish the eventual depth of reception; often this becomes associated with some vaguely deeper taste for literature, especially poetry, and leaves the curious being so disposed a classicist rather than a scholar in English or, indeed, in the other more accessible modern languages. I know that I owe more to Dicky for my love and knowledge of Greek and Latin than to anyone who ever taught me afterward. Which would mean, if true—and I believe it is true— that the experience of a boy of ten to fifteen of a schoolteacher settled things for me in a way which could not be disturbed by far more qualified teachers later.

This was perhaps due somewhat to the nature of teacher and pupil. I was by nature very given to admire and follow someone idiosyncratic in authority, possessed by intense, observable enthusiasm, but also vulnerable. Dicky, in turn, was hardly capable of sensibly discriminating between the enthusiasm of a child for a subject he himself cared for so deeply, and the intelligent appreciation of someone much older. Many years later I heard that Dicky had been retired, a little prematurely, from his former schoolmastership because of a suspicion of pederasty. I certainly know that he never gave any overt, much less harassing, sign of it in relation to me or his other pupils at St. Stephen's Green school. I think it is possible that he felt, and awakened in his students, a depth of emotional attachment which may have originated in the side of his character that had caused him trouble in the past.

Stephen's Green was a snobbish school, niggardly in what it provided intellectually, with only one startling advantage over the larger secondary Protestant or Catholic schools. It frequently hired oddities like Dicky Wood or an ex-parson, A. C. Benson, to teach Greek and Latin and English; and if they were short of masters, they would hire students doing classical Honors in Trinity, far on in their careers. All such people were, in literature anyway, more inspiring than most steady regulars worn down by years and years of highly specialized drudgery. In my time both

Dicky and Benson were far out of the general run (the sort I met later in St. Andrew's and heard of in High School). They were sophisticated in their love and knowledge of literature and absolutely not committed in their beliefs in the way that Protestant and Catholic clergymen were bound to be. The headmaster was an Irishman called Crawley with a Cambridge degree. He was a creaky and cantankerous autocrat, with a dominating presence and a penetrating meanness about money in his management of the school. It was largely as a result of this latter quality that he took on so many of the best and most idiosyncratic masters. They came cheap, because of troubles in their pasts or something that marked them out from their more regular professional brethren. Unfortunately for everyone concerned, Crawley was getting old, and when I was fourteen he retired, having sold the place to a well-meaning but incompetent Englishman called Steede, who having neither Crawley's good points nor bad ones, ran it into the ground in a matter of five years.

Within a short time we discovered that everything that was good in that school, good in what it taught and the discipline necessary to maintain it, had depended on the personality of Crawley. Discipline almost vanished; the older masters vanished through death or retirement; the new headmaster had no knack for finding replacements. I saw incredible scenes of real student violence—a master overpowered by his class and put into the wastepaper basket—and the bullying was something horrible. The master who suffered at the hands of his class was an unsympathetic character and a bit of a bully himself, but when I last saw him he had his trousers taken off and was being kicked around by the class, which unluckily for him contained four or five especially large and strong sixteen-year-olds. It made a lasting impression on me, almost entirely centered on the victimization of the helpless individual. It did not matter really that he was an unpleasant man. In fact he never did much that went beyond pettiness and arrogance. But his humiliation, and just that, was the joyful object of his numerous assailants. Later in Germany and Austria I saw the deliberate enlistment of the hatred and sadism inherent in people, particularly in the young, by an organized government. Self-righteous talk about justice or the vindication of wrongs reproduces exactly the same enthusiasm which annihilates regard for the victim as a fellow creature. Of course what I saw in Stephen's Green was a minor matter, involving nothing worse than a beating up. There was plenty worse to see later on. York (the victim's name) disappeared and was seen no more. The headmaster noticed the disorder in a long speech about behaving like gentlemen. He did not try to discover the identity of the offenders—which would have risked too much in his already rickety school. Shortly after, I left Stephen's Green for the larger and more regular St. Andrew's, where the discipline was intact and the teaching much more orthodox, and I was to stay there till I took my entrance exam for Trinity College.

For a boy of my class in the years between the two world wars, the question of what to do with yourself, with your life in the ordinary world, started several years before you left your private secondary school. "Class" is perhaps the most embracing word for the way I had lived and been brought up; a Protestant, a poor member of the Anglo-Irish middle class, with inevitably a genteel background vaguely associated with past landowning, and certainly even more vaguely associated with being of some importance in Irish society. But the really significant element was the want of money. A recent author rather wittily described the better-paid members of the Anglo-Irish as slightly more than a class and less than a nation. But professional people or business owners in cities and those few landowners who still owned enough land and had enough skill to know what to do with it were a different kind of being from us. We belonged to a much lower order of the population financially, but always reaching somewhat above this, with the sense of and hope of being slightly different.

For the like of myself there was a strictly limited number of options. The most sensible for a boy of some intellectual qualities needing to earn a living as soon as possible in order to relieve his parents—who had had little enough to live on themselves—was to become a bank clerk and to do so straight from school at about sixteen. Places in banks were awarded on the basis of examination in all the regular school subjects. That was one option and that which was most often availed of in St. Andrew's. Another prospect opened at this stage if you either had the small sum of money necessary for tuition at Trinity College or the National University of Ireland, or could earn enough to pay the tuition and keep some over to feed yourself while living at home. You could then enter college as a Pass student (of which more later), and after completing the four undergraduate years earn a B.A., which would open the door to a business or professional career.

I did not have any money of my own to pay fees. Therefore I did consider the possibility of earning my way through. I know of one boy about my age—sixteen or thereabouts—who was left fatherless. His father had been a well-known Dublin solicitor, and it was to everyone's intense surprise to find out at the time of his sudden death that he had left no money at all. Through the kindness of his father's partners this boy was taken on in the lawyers' office as a kind of office boy. He tried and succeeded in getting his B.A. degree by the time he was twenty, took a further law degree, and set up for himself as a solicitor. The remarkable thing is that he made a fairly good living in this way, but for his own pleasure became an art expert and a sort of literary critic. He told me himself many years afterward that his heroic efforts had cut him out of all the more civilized ways of growing up that a proper academic education encouraged. I am afraid he was right. I am certainly glad I did not engage in this proceeding which matched time with such deadly economy against achievement, and left nothing over for either thinking or enjoyment. Nobody could entice me to become a bank clerk—and I am quite sure no bank in its right mind would have given me any encouragement even if I had done well on their examination, which would have been unlikely, since I knew almost no mathematics. As my other options were more or less closed, as I have explained, the only road left me to get into a university was to win an entrance scholarship to either Trinity College (the nominally Protestant university) or University College (the national, heavily Catholic one).

St. Andrew's was supremely concerned about these scholarship exams, for its reputation and therefore the number of its students depended very heavily on them. What was most significant, it seems to me now, is that we were being groomed and trained for Honors in college and nothing else. When you came into Trinity you could in theory take one of two broadly defined courses, Pass or Honors. But the Pass students were all outclassed by those who had entered with the extra amount of specialization demanded by those last two years of school. Without this, and without the high-pressure "education" behind it, the average student had no hope of winning high places in the Honors exams and thereby winning the money as prizes that kept us going. Some students who entered with money of their own and did not need the prizes took the exams or did not, more or less at their discretion. These were often excellent students; one or two whom I knew became good university professors afterward. But for most of us our course both in the last years of school and the four of college were training for either British Civil Service or teaching in university, or in rare cases, in exceptionally highly rated schools.

8

Trinity College

TRINITY AND CLASSICS

The entrance scholarship for Trinity was called Sizarship, and I worked for my last two years in school for the Sizarship examination in classics. "Sizes" was the word used in seventeenth-century English for the food and general subsistence given to students too poor to enter college by any other means. They got this privilege by the intervention of a patron or by examination. They went ahead with their studies like the other boys, but they had to do some of what were servants' jobs. Oliver Goldsmith was a Sizar. The rooms in which he lived are still in what is called Botany Bay (not the most desirable of the blocks of College buildings), though the modern Botany Bay has, needless to say, been much improved and largely rebuilt. In my time it still enjoyed a dubious reputation. It was shabbier than most other "rooms" and noisier, and on the whole the poorer students still lived there.

Sizarship had, however, come a long way up in the world by 1930 over what it had been for Goldsmith. We still got our meals free on Commons, and we paid no fees. But gone were any menial duties, and we won the award solely on examination. All of us who took the examination were subject to a strict means test (that is, our parents were), but the results of the exam were all graded regardless of this and the grades reported. The successful boys whose means exceeded the very low amount demanded were formally listed as winners, but they did not get any of the material awards. Winning Sizarship has thus become a great matter of prestige, instead of a decently intended charity as it had been for Goldsmith.

Tuition therefore was no longer a worry for all four years. But Sizarship awarded no money to live off, nor residential privileges. These had to be earned by other exams. Exam-taking through all of my college career was a thriving industry. Indeed it was very much like earning a small living in the world outside college; but at least you were earning that living by doing what you wanted to do, reading the books you wanted to read (as well as those the College bade you read) and growing up in a more congenial setting than many of us were probably ever going to have again.

When I took Sizarship it was in Greek and Latin literature. I also took an exam in all the other school subjects, but one's special subject counted twice—once for Sizarship and once for the other exam, which was called Junior Exhibition. If you were among the students from all Ireland who competed for Junior Exhibition and if you won, you got twenty-five pounds a year for the first two years. If sometime in the first three years of your career you competed for University Scholarship, you got more money—and you got rooms in college for a very cheap rate indeed. To enter on this long-continued series of steps, each one associated with a massive mustering of all the given knowledge (practically all verbal or linguistic), was rather formidable. But the knowledge that paved one's way upward was ultimately a schoolboy's knowledge. There is ferocious power in a schoolboy's obsessive struggle for something he passionately believes he wants, when he has not yet enough natural development of his appetites (sexual or otherwise) to stand in the way of his frenzied and limited ambitions.

Ruthless and narrow-minded specialization and constant emphasis on examinations started in secondary school. In the curriculum of my last two years of school, science was not compulsory. I was interested to notice latterly that the Homeric scholar Bernard Knox mentions in his autobiography that in his secondary school (which was in England and better than mine) he also escaped any form of scientific instruction during his last two years. That this should have been so seems almost impossible now, but such are the facts. In Ireland, for those of us who were concentrating on Greek and Latin, there was almost no mathematics either. We were being groomed for a very tough race, exactly like racehorses, and any activity which took time away from the main object was shelved. Similarly, those specializing in math or science did not have to do any work in classics. Of course, since all the specialists were also going to compete with each other for Junior Exhibition, we all tried to do a little nibbling at other school subjects that interested us and could be got with very little involvement in extra assignments. I did very well in French and English, history and geography in the exam, though I did exceedingly little work in those subjects during my last two years in school. They were just areas in which to plunder extra marks, enough to carry one into the ranks of the winners.

The men who taught Honors Classics in Trinity College had enough of the unusual and exotic to furnish a mysterious element to our education. They were nearly all of the recognizable British eccentric type, something grown much rarer since. There were five or six of them lecturing, or teaching if one preferred that title, and at least three of them—the seniors of the group—combined a well-deserved reputation for scholarship, backed up by a fair amount of scholarly publication, with a remoteness from ordinary life, and manifest loneliness, and very notably an inability to act or speak or dress like any normal members of their class and kind.

There was J. G. Smyly, one of the leading papyrologists of his day. Literary and other texts in Greek were preserved on papyrus for many hundreds of years before people came to use the expensive calfskin and other materials. But papyrus was not very lasting, and most of what has come down to us in papyrus is fragmentary. Indeed, many of the papyrus fragments are not literary at all. An unkind classicist vexed at the intrusion of the archaeologists once angrily discounted the value of learning from the contents of "thousands of washerwomen's bills in Egypt." Smyly and the two Oxford scholars B. P. Grenfell and A. S. hunt had edited a huge body of this material, called the Tebtunis papyri. At the time I came to college Smyly was temporarily doing a job that he found slightly uncomfortable. The professor who was responsible for Indo-European Comparative Philology had died, and the exam paper in the subject, which was always a part of Scholarship in classics—a very difficult and extensive exam in the middle of the Honors classical course—had to be set by someone, and lectures given as a preliminary. Smyly was taken out of retirement for the purpose because of the enormous knowledge of rare Greek words which he had picked up from his readings in the papyri. These words tended to be useful for explaining the various shifts in sound and form in the evolution of the comparative philology process. Smyly certainly knew something about the theoretical side of comparative philology—mostly Antoine Meillet's seminal text of the midtwenties, *Introduction à l'étude comparative des langues indo-européennes*—but he made quite fascinating the use of the rare words to illustrate Meillet. He made me feel a passionate, almost romantic, interest in comparative linguistics because of his own odd approach.

In the early 1930s Smyly looked like a photograph of a gentleman of the 1880s: stiff round collar, full morning dress, and an immense head of white hair framing a face which suggested an old eagle. He was reputed to be a prince—or whatever the proper honorific title—in the order of the Masons; his presence was certainly steeped in aristocratic dignity. I remember the shock that ran through the class when he cited, as an example, the Greek word *epibda* from Pindar, which there means the consequences of overindulgence in drinking. Smyly translated it for us as "You might say, ladies and gentlemen, the headache of the morning after." Somehow, everything was out of kilter—the pompous address (we were all about eighteen), the formality of the words and the dress, and the appeal to us in a colloquial reference which was supposed, quite wrongly, to put us at our ease with him. He was also a librarian of the College, and a somewhat remiss librarian.

His own main interests were music and pornography, and books connected with these subjects were carefully attended to. I was told by his successor that he found boxes and boxes of volumes treating other subjects that had never been unpacked. He used to play the violin within hearing distance of those of us who used the reading room of the Old Library, and to us he seemed to play extremely well.

There was George Mooney, who had just changed from being University Professor of Latin to the Regius Professor of Greek. Being Mooney, his main contributions during his Latin professorship were two uniquely valuable editions of Apollonius and of the *Alexandra* of Lycophron, two late Greek poets; and he celebrated his elevation to the chair of Greek (the senior of the two professorships) by editing Suetonius's *Lives of the Caesars,* an especially important Latin text. As a human being everything marked him as inaccessible. Extremely reserved and shy, his physical features were unusually off-putting. He had only one eye—the other had been lost in his early days out hunting—and the missing eye was unabashedly just what it was, without a shade or anything else. He had a husky, sepulchral voice which he used very little. His clothes were always in rags. He was a very severe examiner on texts, being notorious for setting as "unseens" (that is, sections which were not on the prescribed parts of the author studied) passages which were themselves extremely hard even with commentaries and lexicon. In such an exam paper the difficulty was obvious and his markings niggardly. But all that was clear and straightforward; however, he also administered vivas (orals) in particular texts prescribed. On Scholarship he had two vivas, one on the *Iliad* and the *Odyssey* and the other on Thucydides, book 7. He apparently assessed us by some private standard of his own which had little to do with the questions he asked and we answered. He examined in Scholarship every year for a number of years, and for some extraordinary reason always asked the same questions on his viva. These questions were always quite particular, and as Scholarship was a very difficult exam it was often taken by the same candidate two or three times before getting it—or giving up taking it. Consequently many students knew exactly the questions he was going to ask them. But seemingly Mooney quickly decided either that you had read the books thoroughly when you answered or you had merely been told what his questions were. If the latter, he gave you three or four marks out of ten automatically. I remember sitting alongside him at a desk as he glanced at me with his good eye and said, "Lad, do you know the description of Olympus in the *Odyssey?*" I did know that this was one of Mooney's pet questions and had learned it by heart. Then there was an uncomfortable silence which he broke by asking, "Do you know what word Homer uses for a worm?" (He made the keyword a double syllable—"wor-um.") This one I had not heard about, but fortunately remembered that indeed there were two: one, the worms that might have but hadn't eaten Odysseus's bow; the other, the "gleaming worms" that had been kept from eating Hector's body by the gods' intervention. Mooney made a very slight movement, and I knew that something had happened. He then asked me a number of detailed questions on readings, etc., and then quite unexpectedly made me talk about what I thought was the role of Laertes in the *Odyssey,* a discussion in which he joined with evident pleasure. "That will do, lad," he said, and it was over. He gave me eight marks out of a possible ten. I lost the other two, I think, for knowing the description of Olympus by heart, palpably by having been told of it beforehand.

I have not forgotten a most unexpected bit of kindness from Mooney. I was taking the exam for the Vice Chancellor's Medals. For that, in the year I took it, the text was the entire body of Terence's plays, all six of them, with three papers of passages for translation into English, a mass of exegetical questions, and finally a verse composition in the style and meter of Terence based on a given scene of Shakespeare. Mine was one of the Nurse's exhortations to Juliet. It was great fun doing this, no matter how absurd it is now made to look by more serious scholars.

The exam was always held in the Examination Hall, in those days without central heating or electricity. The month was November. I had six hours of writing the first day and six the second. I wore my overcoat with my gown on top and thin gloves on my hands. On the second morning of the exam Mooney entered with his printed exam paper in his hand—the College Press always printed the exams then, Greek characters and all, with your examiner's name at the top. The exam was sealed in an envelope which the said examiner broke open before your eyes. Mooney took one look at me and growled out, "Can you think of any reason why you should take this exam in this ghastly place?" I couldn't, so he beckoned me to follow him and put me in his rooms with a blazing fire and a cup of tea. It may not seem like much now, but then it was very different. He so rarely spoke to any of us at all and did not seem to notice much. The unexpected kindness was quite overwhelming, all the more so because the other two examiners, who always gave the impression of noticing students more, had passed by several times on the previous day in that chilly hall without passing any comment.

Then there was Sir Robert Tate, knighted for his services as an interpreter to the forces during World War I. He also had a Distinguished Service Order, so I assume he had done some fighting, too. He apparently knew ten to fifteen languages as well as his Greek, Latin and Hebrew. I have been told by his well-wishers, as well as their opposites, that he spoke all the modern languages with perfect correctness and an impeccable Anglo-Irish accent. He used to teach us how to write Greek and Latin prose and verse. He would, for instance, on Tuesday give us a passage of any author from Milton to Wordsworth, and on the following Tuesday take up our versions of them, done into whatever meter you deemed appropriate—hexameters for Milton, Ovidian or Tibullan elegiacs for Wordsworth. No one was compelled to send in versions, I secretly believe that the very harsh criticism to which we were subjected by Sir Robert was partly designed to diminish the number of copies given him to read. On the Thursday following he would enter the classroom, sit down with his face ostentatiously away from us and toward the window and lawn in the Square. He would then catalogue our infelicities or downright blunders without attributing any of them by name to the unhappy listening faces which would begin to redden. He would then comment with something like this: "I say nothing about the poetry of this;

it is too much to expect that you have enough feeling for English poetry to have any notion of how to render it in Latin or Greek—but at least you ought to know the simple rules of Latin and Greek meter." I remember how I once glowed with delight when he read my version through, saying nothing at first. He then remarked, "I don't say this is good—but it's not at all bad; but I don't like the last couplet. It has the wrong ring to it for Ovid." About three weeks later I was at a college dance and there was Sir Robert—who was a deservedly well-known dancer. During an intermission he walked over to me and quoted two lines from Ovid and said, "You see what I mean, my dear fellow; that's why your lines seemed wrong."

These three were, as I have said, a breed that has grown very scarce. Some time ago I had a conversation with a professor of the College whom I had known since childhood days. He said that it had taken him a long time to realize that these eccentrics had been made so by suffering and frustration, and that was good for nobody. I don't know; but I do know that each of these men made very notable written contributions to the exegetical and stylistic values of classical literature. What is more, there is something special in being taught classics by men whom you cannot possibly imagine as being really like yourself when they were young. They come before you as a part of the mystery that lies in their complete mastery of those long-dead languages, and in their eerie power to jolt your imagination beyond almost anything that you can read of criticism in the more modern and apparently commonsensical fashion. It is true of course that they were dealing with works that inflame the imagination, so that it is hard to think it possible that you would not be engaged, with Homer and Herodotus, with Thucydides and the tragedies, with Lucretius, Vergil, and Tacitus. But it is better, I believe, if those who teach you do so from the heart of their own perhaps twisted personality, rather than with the standardized presentation of new historical evidence or current theories of psychology or anthropology. At any rate, there was some sort of inner harmony between the isolation and complexity of their personalities and their nearly magical way of understanding the texts and rendering them alive again in living linguistic detail.

By the circumstances of my life, geographically and historically—between Ireland, very briefly Vienna, and then mostly America, both in schooling and in teaching—I have lived through a tremendous change in the evolution of classical studies in Western culture. The old educational order which emerged from the sixteenth to the nineteenth centuries across the continent of Europe rested heavily on the instructional value of the classics in history, philosophy, literature, and morality. This was especially the case in nineteenth-century Britain, where classics became a training ground for an elite selected to govern the British Empire. It seems astonishing to me now that as late as my undergraduate days in the early 1930s the Indian Civil Service was stocked exclusively from candidates who had passed a single examination, a general paper, and an interview. The exam was really a repetition of your final Honors exam in your special subject at the university. Classics was strongly favored, and a very large number of those who went on to govern the Empire had received nearly everything that was important in their education from their classical studies. After being passed for the Empire service, the successful candidate spent a year or so at the government's expense learning a little law and whatever language seemed appropriate to where he was being sent. I distinctly remember dining, late in my undergraduate career, with a man who was the chief judicial authority in Burma only ten years after getting a first-class Honors degree in Classical Moderatorship, which I was to do myself a year later. The idea of employing someone for an important administrative position with almost no technical preparation is not one welcome to modern democratic governments today. But, by what evidence one can come by, the system seems to have worked surprisingly well. On a recent trip to India, a casual observer like myself every day encountered strong praise —tinged with slight regret at its passing—for the general legal administration of British India. It was certainly not a system in which justice was corrupted in its court administration, although it was often ignorantly implemented. And the fact remains that the entire Indian legal system is based on that established by the Raj.

But the most remarkable feature of classical training in my time was its obdurately philological character. This was much less so in France and Germany, where university professors paid much more than lip service to the content of Greek and Latin literature. Within such a specific context, our Irish professors certainly concerned themselves almost exclusively with the verbal and stylistic aspects of the languages studied (and the same was, as far as I can find out, largely true in England). In their publications these same interests took precedence. A few of these teachers and professors, I suppose, were a kind of barbarian, but not most of them. They felt that classics in itself was something quite different from literature, philosophy, or history. It was a study of a world of its own. In fact, I recently saw this very phrase in a speech by Professor Tom Mitchell, the present provost of Trinity College Dublin. The greater philologists of the old order penetrated deeper than most scholars with the power of an imagination awakened by an endless attention to, and absorption of, the minutest aspects of words of well-known texts in Greek and Latin. These classical texts are not exactly like those in modern languages, where contemporary usage is continually revising and rendering more exact our knowledge of the words, and where there is always more literature coming into existence to modify one's understanding of what has already been read. The Greek and Latin classics, frozen in expression, are beyond further contemporary modification. There is a sense, of course, in which there is a line stretching from Homer through the Greek language of the fifth and fourth centuries to Koine, the language of the New Testament, and then to Byzantine, and finally modern Greek. But Koine and the later forms of the language are not ancient Greek, even in the way in which Chaucer is subsumed into modern English.

There was also a deliberate circumscription of Greek texts, apparently for schoolbooks, going back to Hellenistic times. The selection continued and became the basis of the classics when they were studied during the Renaissance. A similar circumscription in Latin gives one Plautus and Terence, Lucretius, Cicero, Vergil, Ovid, Livy, Tacitus—all the way to Augustine. These two selected bodies of authors merged into a curious self-contained whole in the West, which has seen them in this light for hundreds of years. This entirety became, in effect, a series of contributions to a liturgy rather than a number of truly separate writers. Nowadays, there is a distinct effort to see the classical projection as a field for comparative studies in anthropology or linguistic disciplines. But the period of classical studies between the nineteenth and early twentieth centuries knew nothing of all this. Their attitude truly was toward a kind of liturgy, and liturgies achieve their effects by being learned (by heart if necessary) and forcing themselves into the obscurer parts of the mind and emotions. As a result, in the devotion, love, and veneration of the actual words of the texts, something has come alive in the culture of the West that cannot, I think, be put totally to sleep or lost. That is what the old British Civil Service wanted of their applicants—a certain cast of mind.

After that was attained, the authorities thought it possible to fill that mind with various sorts of special aptitudes. But something imaginative of the greatest consequence came through the absorption of the liturgy and was the prime material out of which the useful elements would grow superimposed. The casualties were, as Gilbert Murray seems to have said, the many students who came to hate the subject because of the way it was taught and the manner in which it was examined; it constantly denied them the chance to see the books as a commentary on, or an extension of, their own kind of lives, as in fact modern literature seemed more fitted to do.

My own case is a mixed one. I am one of the last living products of the older training. There are times when I feel that was fortunate for me because I was a late developer, and I doubt that in my early twenties I could have effectively dealt with the challenge to passion and mind in those classical texts—all the matters that I now press on my American students' attention. I was perhaps better served by the relentless Talmudism of my teachers, as far as my future career went, than I would have been by what now

The Classical Society of Trinity College Dublin, 1931-32.
David is in the top row at the left

appears to be a much more enlightened approach. At the end of eight years in school and four more undergraduate years in college, I had come to know rather well, even if in a peculiar and some people would say distorted fashion, the languages and the texts of Greek and Latin literature. And the method in which I had been taught was to carry me on for scores of years afterward when reading for my own advantage rather than thinking of my pupils. It has made a great difference to my translations, and it has given substance to the freshness of my understanding of Greek and Latin that followed my starting all anew at the University of Chicago. The old British model was on its deathbed anyhow. Willy-nilly, modern teachers of classics have to give instruction much nearer in form to that of modern literature and history. One simple fact made this imperative, if nothing else did. Clearly, it is no longer possible in modern schools to allow enough time to learn the two ancient languages to the complete exclusion of the scores of new subjects crowding for the pupils' attention. The present result is, it appears to me, satisfactory. The books of that ancient world are being used for the purpose which all books surely have: to make direct contact with their readers—and to change them. I am glad to believe that perhaps I do not make disgruntled as many students as the old system did. But I am heartily thankful for having lived inside it and seen its mystery.

THE STUDENTS

Trinity College was a man's world with certain special features that I was never to see again, at least in their original dimensions. There were female students, of course: I should say with some distrust of the accuracy of my memory perhaps 20 percent of the whole. These, in the area of humane letters, were very much in evidence in modern languages. I cannot entirely account for this, but personally I knew a number of daughters of marriages where either mother or father was a native speaker of French, German, Italian, or Spanish. I remember a professor (and of philosophy, too) saying that he distrusted results in modern languages because the students were mostly women and moreover knew the languages in part from childhood. This meant that they were not being tested like those in classics or philosophy. Their being women lent the final touch of unconvincingness to their professional achievement. There were some women in the medical school, mostly specializing in gynecology. There was, surprisingly, one woman professor—of history—though hardly any women students in that school. She certainly was a person of intensely individual personality, and so made it, I suppose.

But the big division amongst the students had a twofold aspect—those that were in the Honors school versus those who were Pass students, and those who "lived in" or did not (i.e., those that had rooms on the campus and those who had not). The two of these distinctions tended to coalesce. Honors students studied only one discipline, say math, or classics, or philosophy (masquerading as Mental and Moral Science), or modern languages. The goal of all these was a Moderatorship in their subject, classed as First, Second, or Third, depending on their aggregate marks at the final exam; numerical marks were always used instead of letter grades. Honors courses in these particular disciplines were totally different from those taken by students who were formally registered as Pass, who studied nearly all the school subjects still. They ended by getting B.A. degrees just the way the Honors students did, but they could not add "Mod.": i.e., B.A. (Mod.) The Pass people became parsons, after doing some work in the Divinity School, or they got jobs as schoolmasters in minor schools, especially if they had athletic abilities. Or they went into business, or into professional training as doctors, lawyers, or engineers. The "Hons" people, at least those who got Firsts, ended up in academic posts or the civil service (British).

Huge as the difference was between Pass and Honors, both in the kind of students taking each and in the life they led in college, it was hardly greater than whether one had rooms in college or not. Rooms were not very dear, but everyone was much poorer then, both absolutely and relatively, compared with now. You got rooms at an immensely reduced rate if you were a Scholar of the House. This distinction you won by taking a portentous examination, which in classics covered all the books you had studied or would study in the Honors course from your first day in college to the end of your third year. Philosophy and modern languages Scholarships were awarded on the same basis. Everything was done to make you feel that becoming a Scholar was something permanently valuable. The College is nominally governed by its Fellows and Scholars. You never lose the title of Scholar, and the College stands you one ceremonial banquet every ten years until you die. Naturally, the later honorific occasions are a little uncomfortable psychologically, as you see your contemporaries aging and wonder about yourself. Your Scholarship also awarded you a modest salary of twenty-five pounds a year, together with dinners on Commons and remission of fees, though for people like myself who had won Sizarship on entrance, these last two benefits were already at our disposal.

One result of this system was that those of you who lived in *and* specialized in this way were all competing elitists; and a group of the various elitists who chose one another out of disinterested friendship was very elitist indeed. In fact you were a little community all on your own, and you barely knew that the rest of the college existed. The modern language Scholars, being mostly women, could not live in college because of the six o'clock rule, which banished women from college property after that hour. (They got extra salary benefits to compensate them for this denial of privileges.) This separation of the sexes was not an arrangement peculiar to Trinity; it was the same in Oxford and Cambridge, and it is less than thirty years since it was decisively altered in all three institutions. Its evident unnaturalness was, even in my time, resented, but despite a number of isolated protests it held out.

It sometimes seems hard to speak truthfully about a sexual revolution; since it is an area so loaded with the most powerful impulses, I find myself, with others, saying things like: "Probably under the wraps, everything was very much the same always." Well, it isn't true. And one reason I know it isn't true is because I briefly belonged to this society which had to be changed by something which can only be truly described as a sexual revolution. There we were, eighteen to twenty-two, of course intensely sexually concerned, with almost no simple or unconstrained way of living sexually. Being in company with clever and handsome women at classes and elsewhere in Dublin, of course we fell in love. One had women friends with whom one went to the theater or shared meals—outside. But almost all the women lived at home, which was the usual thing to do then, or at separate women's college apartments three miles from Trinity itself. In almost no circumstances could one bring them into college rooms. We none of us owned cars. I recollect a passage in *Dubliners* in which Joyce has one of his *dramatis personae* notice the discomfort of the damp and cold of the grass in Phoenix Park, and his disgust and disturbance at the figures wrapped in sensual embraces there. It's all true. There was another such haunt called Nutley Lane. It sometimes still amuses me when I am in Dublin to drive by it. It is now row on row of immensely respectable middle-class houses. Then it was a small lane between two thoroughfares. These were at times the necessitous alternatives to chastity. They were not very attractive alternatives.

One very daring innovation in the prevailing system, allowed only after an application to the junior dean, was permission to have a female student to tea in your rooms. Even this was often not to be had without the disguise of a small party of other men and women. Of course, one had to warn the rest off, apart from your particular "guest." The whole thing caused the maximum degree of arrangement and embarrassment, and an absurd kind of secrecy and ambiguity. I have heard people of my generation say (but long afterward) that it was romantic and stimulating. I disagree. It was absurd and damaging.

It is curious that there was very little homosexuality. I suppose it is difficult to make this statement with any positive degree of proof; but for what it is worth I believe it is true. What there certainly was, was an intense intellectual life shared by small groups of men friends who met in the rooms of one of us night after night, mostly when the library reading room closed after 10:00 p.m., and drank tea or occasionally whiskey or gin till 2:00 or 3:00 a.m. I think the most stimulating part of my education came from those discussions: on the traditional topics of God, freedom, and immortality, but above all else on the books that embodied the knowledge of these matters. Far the most of the books we discussed were in modern languages, and naturally in English. Dickens, Conrad, and Hardy; Tolstoy and Dostoyevsky in translation; Flaubert and Stendhal, usually in French; and a great deal of Irish poetry and drama, in which we felt an excited possessiveness. Only very gradually did those of us who studied in the classical school come to think of and talk about our authors. We had been so forced to think in linguistic and exegetical terms, and anyhow we were only beginning to ask ourselves the vital questions which affected our lives and sympathies as human beings; so we literally found it hard to formulate such questions in regard to the Greek and Latin texts where no one had ever bothered to push for our opinions of how these writers represented them. But I remember the awakening, which was first for me in Homer, where the poetry lies so open to apprehension even in Greek, that I surrendered to it as certainly as I had already to Milton. And then Herodotus and Thucydides, and Aeschylus among the dramatists. Latin came later; but Lucretius and Tacitus early in *that* list. Of course we were very little examined in such aspects of the classical literature, but once we were launched into our own appreciation of it I think we were, at times anyhow, glad of having it as our personal possession, a private thing untouched by professional (i.e., examinational) concern.

TRINITY AND IRELAND

When I came up to Trinity College in 1930 it was, as a political institution, in the very last phase of what it had been since its foundation by Elizabeth I in 1592. We the students certainly did not understand this, and I rather doubt that the government of the College understood it either. When Trinity was founded it was intended to be somewhat like a Cambridge or Oxford college: that is, as one of several small, independent educational bodies composing the University of Dublin. For many reasons which would take too long to recapitulate, this did not happen. Trinity remained the only college, something much too big as a single college in comparison with "Oxbridge" colleges, and somewhat small to be a university in itself. Yet it did formally retain both titles. There were about twelve hundred students, nearly all undergraduate. To this day graduate students are a minority. Professors were formally professors of the University of Dublin, but the Fellows, appointed for life, were Fellows of Trinity College. Originally, all Fellows had to be Protestant clergymen and, officially anyhow, celibate. Until the 1850s this rule obtained, and there was a very steady movement of Fellows out of Trinity and into the church as bishops, archdeacons, and so on. This kept the faculty comparatively young—and the governing body of the College, consisting of Fellows and two of the professors, was reasonably young too. (The celibacy was largely a fraud, and the babies born to Dr. Brown, Fellow, and Miss Smith failed to raise a scandal.) But when the celibacy rule and the restriction of fellowship to Protestant clergymen were abolished, the lifeblood no longer ran so quickly in the collegiate veins. The Fellows stayed on and on, and the governing board had an average age of close to seventy to eighty in my time. They were buttressed and safe, and usually very loyal to the college, but such a huge preponderance of old men naturally precluded any very daring advances in College policy.

By then very few of the board lived in college, though they kept their rooms in it still. I remember well the huge black limousines, on Saturday mornings during the academic year, bringing our governors to confer and decide the destiny of Trinity. I remember, also well, a conversation I had with McCann, the mace bearer (familiarly known as the Blue Bottle) when I said to him how shaky they looked as their chauffeurs got them out of the cars in the Front Square. He agreed and said, "When the wind is east we don't bring the old gentlemen in but postpone the meeting till another more clement day."

The College under Elizabeth I, and indeed until the takeover by the Irish National government in 1921, was designed to produce reliable leaders of Irish society under the British mandate. It was heavily Anglo-Irish ethnically and also fairly Protestant, though not exclusively; the Anglo-Irish were those descended from the English who came to Ireland from about 1600 on, and they mostly tended to remain as a scattered but distinct minority social group and to marry within it. However, several Anglo-Irish/Protestant graduates of Trinity were also important in the ranks of the Irish nationalists. In 1921 the Anglo-Irish, conspicuous by their English names, held more than 50 percent of the main medical, law, and banking jobs in Ireland. But this proportion was clearly bound to shift. The changes that occurred after this, took place with much less violence and intolerance than might reasonably have been expected. The trend toward a predominantly Catholic middle-class majority in these positions of authority happened in a way that could fairly be described as natural and moderate, and by the end of the forties the change was decisive.

Also, the Land Acts which began under the British government of the early 1880s were intensified with greater impetus in the 1920s. Under these acts, where there was a demand for land in a given county, farms of twenty-five to thirty acres were formed and financed in long-term loans by the government. The land came by compulsory purchase—but perfectly fair purchase—from the large estates, the latter markedly the possession of Anglo-Irish Protestants. Thus the Anglo-Irish population was bound to decline. Over and above those who lost much of their land, the Anglo-Irish propertied class was discouraged, and great numbers of them went to England.

With these changes, the hope was that we might have a more unified Ireland in which the origins of its own citizens would no longer be subject to discrimination as Anglo-Irish or pure "native" Irish. Trinity should therefore go ahead with any policy which recognized us as a leading Irish university, somehow coordinate with National University of Ireland, our Catholic rival.

One problem was that for a long time there had been a good deal of strong Catholic opposition to Trinity as a "garrison" university. Successive Catholic archbishops of Dublin (including John McQuaid, who held the post through 1971) told Catholic parents within their diocese that they were in danger of mortal sin if they sent their children to Trinity College—something which it turns out they had absolutely no theological right to do. But when in the course of time McQuaid vanished from the scene, the Catholic archbishop of Armagh and head of Catholicism in Ireland, Cardinal Conway, was appealed to to regularize the position; and after some initial cautious moves he gave way and the ban was removed. This was certainly better, and it is the course that has been followed since, so that it is hardly possible now to establish any striking difference between the two Dublin colleges in point of their students' ethnic or religious affiliations. However, both universities now exist thanks to government grants, and that means that they are intensely subject to governmental pressure. Trinity and National both are dreadfully overcrowded; and the kinds of students entering, and the subjects they will study, are greatly influenced by the central government.

In 1930 we felt a tolerance for the new direction, but without much enthusiasm and without any satisfaction as to where the prospects were going to appear for the educated, predominantly Protestant elite in Ireland. At the same time, by the middle thirties the handwriting was on the wall for the Empire, which had always absorbed many of those who graduated from Trinity with Honors degrees, especially in the humanistic subjects. Southern Ireland, then as now, had a bit more than three million people. There was and is simply no way to find employment for the comparatively large percentage of educated citizens.

Much of the political ambience of the college was still tenaciously and somewhat amusingly backward. The classical dons, Sir Robert Tate and Frank Godfrey, still referred to one another—only half-humorously—as Major Tate and Captain Godfrey, as indeed they had been in the 1914-18 war. This was simply a sentimental gesture, but one needs to remember that on November 11 every year we commemorated the thousands of Irishmen all over the country, and in our case the twelve or thirteen hundred students of Trinity, who had died under the banners of the famous old Irish regiments of the British Army—the South Irish Horse, the Dublin Fusiliers, etc. Thirty thousand Irishmen died in that war in comparison with the mere handful of hundreds that died in the Rebellion of 1916 and the Irish war of independence in 1919-21.

A party around 1934 stands out in my memory. There was a group of fifteen or twenty of us, including some faculty, e.g., Sir Robert (Major) Tate and also a young visiting German lecturer. We had all been drinking and later in the evening started singing national anthems. We sang our "new" national anthem—"Amhrán na bhFiann" (The Soldier's Song)—with a certain tipsy irreverence, and Sir Robert stood to his feet, though with a slight reluctance. After this we sang "God Save the King," and Sir Robert clearly enjoyed that. But the most remarkable case was our German lecturer (remember, the date is 1934, early in the Hitler era). He had probably drunk more than all the rest of us, but when "Deutschland über Alles" rang out he started to his feet, stood *stramm*, and sang with all the seriousness of religious devotion. As the song ended, dear old Sir Robert approached the German and extended his hand, saying, "My dear fellow, if there had been more like you, the war would never have happened" (i.e., WWI).

This was the mood against the background of which most of us lived. We were much less sentimental than our elders, who genuinely felt the ties between Ireland and England, but we lived in great doubtfulness about our future and leaned toward going somewhere else—not in Ireland. Most of us had country backgrounds or ties with the Irish countryside—walking, shooting, fishing, or hunting. We were deeply in love with Ireland visually experienced, with her endlessly changing skies and their subtle ambiguities. Also with her ordinary people, mostly country people. Yet we were separated from Irishness in the sense that an Englishman or a Frenchman of any kind or class would still feel English or French. But we certainly did not feel English: a week's stay in London would convince any one of us of that. It was not that we disliked the English. It was just that we were not English—less English than we were even Irish.

Yes, the Trinity of that day was frozen, both in its institutional life and in its political position. But if one wants to understand something about modern Ireland, it was an advantage to have seen such elements of the leadership of Irish society as still survived between 1930 and 1948; and to have seen the remnant outline of the old Trinity, the Anglo-Irish and the Protestant Ascendancy. The college was in those years still uniquely itself; the years of conformity with the red-brick universities of England and many American colleges were still in the future. I feel as if I had lived in the last authentic moments of an era of its history. The Fellows were mainly Anglo-Irish, either chosen by examination, or

later by a process of cooptation by the Fellows in their particular department. Such systems may sometimes be unjust. Still,
I do not see entirely the advantage of the British system which
has replaced these, where you advertise for a staff member in
a certain field, and submit the names of those answering to the
final adjudication of an external assessor from outside one's own
college altogether. This procedure is based on some idea of the
"objective" professional skill of the man or woman to be selected.
But no college lives solely by these merits of its professors; it has
to have a continuing and distinctive intellectual life, and some
thought should surely be given to the suitability of a new addition
to the staff who are there already, and are shaping that life.

9

Vienna

The years in Trinity as an undergraduate were good years and very successful. I did two Mods., one in classics and the other in ancient history and political science, and won what was called Studentship. This was a prize (if I correctly recollect) of a hundred pounds for a year, together with the obligation to teach two Pass courses in classics. But the College also gave me a lectureship in classics. It was tenable for three years, and clearly marked me out as someone they thought of as a possible member of the staff, or even as a Fellow, with its lifetime association with the College. It was a generous tryout for someone so young. But the college I came to know as a junior staff member lacked most of the faces and already some of the atmosphere of the previous four years. I was also beginning to think that I should know how classics was taught elsewhere in Europe. Since at this stage none of us wanted to spend a penny of money that could reach Nazi Germany, I asked my friend George Thomson (author of the best book I know on Greek lyrics, *Greek Lyric Metre*), where he thought I should go. He and his Cambridge colleague (Frank Adcock) suggested that I go to Vienna to study with Ludwig Radermacher. With the kind consent of the Trinity authorities I went off to study in Vienna for about a year.

Radermacher, a Rheinlander, was an excellent teacher, and from him I learned much that was entirely new to me. He taught me how folklore could contribute to one's understanding of Greek comedy. I, in turn, made a real hit with him by reciting the verse sung by Irish boys on St. Stephen's Day:

> The wren, the wren, the king of all birds,
> St. Stephen's Day he was caught in the furze,
> And though he is little his fortune is great,
> So come out good people and give us a trate.

Nowadays, thank God, in place of a wren hunt, a mere representative of the wren is brought out. Still, Radermacher insisted that my performance supported his theory of Tier Masquerade, which showed how folklore indicates various examples of the assumption of the role of animals and birds in primitive rituals. He referred this to Greek comedy—*The Birds, The Frogs,* etc.

I have two other vivid recollections of my time with Professor Radermacher. I participated in his seminar on Longinus's *On the Sublime*, which was conducted in Latin, one of the very last sessions so managed on the Continent, I am told. It was a revelation to me how in this setting speaking Latin, which all of us knew well, was hopelessly clumsy, if not impossible. However, I still think that an important dimension of the language *is* acquired by people who systematically speak Latin. For instance, my colleague in the Committee on Social Thought at the University of Chicago, David Tracy, greatly benefited from speaking Latin in Rome as a novice, even if the quality was sometimes of the order of the American cardinal who declared in a conference, *"haec opinio non tenet aquam"* (this opinion won't hold water). Radermacher also gave a wonderful class on Sophocles' *Philoctetes*—a very sensitive analysis of the play. Perhaps the most important thing of all that he did for me was to show me another way of teaching classics very far from the purely philological approach I knew from Trinity.

I lived in Vienna from March until December 1935. My impressions of the city were both good and ill. There was a notion that Austria in its new and shrunken role after the end of the Austro-Hungarian Empire might have some of the advantages of a relation to German scholarship in classics and none of the political disadvantages. Particularly in the latter aspect this was a much too sanguine view. The Austria of the middle and late thirties was governed by a narrow-minded and oppressive clerical dictatorship that, in such matters as anti-Semitism, was just barely preferable to Nazism.

Apart from Radermacher, the university was a place where you entered in the morning after showing your passport or *carte d'identité* to the armed guards at the door. Two Jewish students had been murdered on university property the year before. The city I found horribly dull, with its emphasis on "Wien blcibt Wien" (Vienna remains Vienna) in all the nightclubs and *cafés chantants*. It was so clearly untrue. There wasn't as much traffic in the streets of this heavily Hapsburg town as would have graced the streets of provincial Limerick at the same period. There was something ponderous about the surviving Hapsburg architecture. There was indeed a wonder in the Stephansdom (twelfth century), but that was a very far cry from nearly everything else, which belonged from 1820 to 1900. My impression was that the Austrians had carried their imperial role very heavily at any time, and now there was nothing left but a shell. The middle classes had lost all their money in the inflation directly following World War I. There was massive unemployment. The bulk of the people and nearly all the students were Nazis, because they could not see (I am afraid they were right) that there was a future for Austria except by an *Anschluss* with Germany. The government was organized by an association called *Vaterlandische Front* (the Patriotic Front), many of whose members were the unfortunate Jews who couldn't get out of the country and knew that the coming of the Nazis would be the end of them. They also knew that they were trusting to a broken reed in this Patriotic Front, but saw nothing else to do. The leaders of the front were more than equivocal figures like Kurt Schuschnigg, Major Tey, and the Prince Ernst Rüdiger von Starhemberg. I have never lived in a city so constantly and inevitably in the grip of depression—no jobs, no money, and a future consisting of nothing but fear.

On the personal side, there were two incidents in Vienna which stick in my mind. They were vaguely connected, in the kind of cause-and-effect relationship that appears and usually is governed by pure chance. The first was trivial and funny, the second of tremendous consequence to me, for it led to my coming to America and eventually to the University of Chicago, and to most of a lifetime spent in its service.

The first happened a few days after my arrival in Vienna. I had learned only fragments of German before arriving in Austria, but I had several introductions to Austrians from Irish friends who had lived there off and on. One was to a rich Romanian family. The mother had divorced her husband and married a very distinguished Viennese doctor. She had a daughter by her first marriage who was studying in Paris, but at this moment was spending brief holidays in Vienna. She was about twenty, very handsome, with fair hair, blue eyes, and a marvelous body. Her mother had two seats for the opera which she did not intend to use and offered them to her daughter and myself. I asked the girl out to dinner ahead of the opera—which was *Parsifal*. We got on famously, though linguistic communication was pretty sketchy. Suzi spoke French easily, German more hesitantly, and English hardly at all. I still knew very little German, but during the few days of my stay I had improved my stock—a lot more than I had expected. I have, or perhaps I had, a knack of picking up a speaking knowledge of languages when there is no alternative. I was living in the Maysedergasse in an apartment in a building where no one spoke any English. My reading French has always been good (I had eight years of it in school), but I had almost no experience of speaking it. We made an odd couple, but during dinner we got better at talking to one another. I spoke German until I stuck, when I tried my clumsy and maladroit French. She rejoined in French very fluently and with a wonderful husky accent which I found enchanting and singularly easy to understand because she spoke slowly. I suppose that had something to do with her native use of

Romanian. We went to the opera in high spirits, and as *Parsifal* dragged its melodramatic length along, there was a real ecstasy in reciprocity of feeling. At the end, almost without invitation or agreement, we went back to my apartment, where we spent a very happy night till about 3 a.m., when I took her home in a taxi. Next morning, my landlady met me with a gloomy face and gave me notice to move out. I said something feeble to the effect that I had not expected her to have such strong views about my having a girl in my rooms. (After all, this was Vienna, about which I had heard much that would never have been true of Dublin.) She got very angry and said of course she would not have objected to a girl. This was a man; she had heard his voice, and that sort of thing she could not tolerate. I changed my rooms, and till Suzi went back to Paris we had no further trouble about the lodging. I could not help reflecting, humorously, that in Dublin under sim-ilar circumstances, my landlady would have unhesitantly thrown me out if she had thought my companion was a girl. I believe, though, that if she had assumed that the offender was a male she would have been very hesitant to do any such thing, because the offense would have been so much beyond anything that she could think likely.

The second incident happened quite fortuitously. Suzi was supposed to be looking forward to my visit to Paris at Easter. Near that time I got a long and garbled telegram explaining why this proved impossible. I knew quite well why; she had picked up someone else. In a fit of indignation and some amusement I tried to think of something else to do with my university vacation that would be novel and exciting. I ended by going to Budapest, and by air. This was the first time I had ever traveled by airplane. In my Budapest pension I met a very nice American middle-aged woman who was in central Europe trying to get a child for adoption. She was a psychoanalyst and fairly wealthy, but she had had no success in her effort. She had found very little to amuse her in Budapest in the past two weeks. I took her out to a gypsy restaurant where there was good music, and the food was good and new to her. When she was going away she told me that when I got back to

Vienna I should ring up a friend of hers whom she had known ever since they were teenagers together. He was a composer—i.e., wrote music—and was married to a psychoanalyst who was a close friend and associate of Freud. Their name was Brunswick, and Mark was, almost providentially, deeply interested in classical literature, though he studied it in English and German. They had lived in Vienna for fourteen or fifteen years. Mark and I met in the Grand Hotel on the Ring and there began a friendship which lasted the rest of his life—another thirty-six years. It all began with eating raw beef sandwiches in that beastly overluxurious hotel. I can still see Mark with his Vandyke beard and restless eyes and ready laugh. He and his wife Ruth made Vienna a very different city for me.

Aside from my work at the university studying under Rader-macher, I had not found much to interest me in the city. But Mark and Ruth Brunswick lived on in Vienna as they had done since the early 1920s, knowing by the turn of the thirties all the risks they ran. They were Jews, but had perhaps some small defense in being U.S. citizens. How much this would avail them, when the Nazis came, looked very doubtful. As things actually happened, Mark was out of the country when the takeover happened. Ruth deliberately stayed on until she and Princess Marie Bonaparte, also a psychoanalyst, and married to Prince George of Greece, induced the Austrian Nazi government to let "Professor" go—the name universally used for Freud in Vienna. The Nazis did so in return for some immense sum in dollars. He went to London, where he died within a couple of years.

It was the way the Brunswicks carried on, with this sword of Damocles hanging over them, that changed my feeling about living in Vienna. At some level it made the city a component of real life, and how they handled it suggested something more worth knowing and living in than I had felt hitherto. The risks and courage involved made the place more alive, as though its faded-ness were not all that there was to it. Besides the affection of Mark and Ruth for myself, the way in which the three of us could enjoy what still remained that was delightful in the city—the boating and bathing in the Danube, the small and good restaurants once one knew of them, the beauty of the Brunswicks' house on the Hasenauerstrasse in Grinzing—all gradually overwhelmed the drabness and plain boredom of my first few months in Vienna. I have never been good at a diet of museums, galleries, the outsides of buildings. In a foreign city nothing significant happens to me until the setting takes me to itself and I can live there in a limited ordinary way. I know nothing about music except folk songs, but I came to love some of Mark's compositions and the concerts they were part of. Mark possessed a huge aviary covering two vast rooms at the top of his house, and he would watch his birds for hours—exotic tropical birds and local German and Austrian ones—just as I used to watch my favorite zoo animals or my own pets in the days of my childhood. He was a somewhat lonely man with few interests, and those he pursued intensely—his music, Greek literature, and his birds. I think it was conversations with Mark which first made me see the value of translations of classical literature—the value that even the most difficult and doubtful translations of Greek poetry could have for a cultivated and intelligent man or woman. This was to open my mind to courses given in translation at the University of Chicago afterward, and to drive me to make as good translations as I could myself. As Radermacher had taught me how Sophocles in Greek could be a part of a discussion just as one might have on Shakespeare, so Mark helped me to realize that much Greek literature could be communicated to those who did not know the language, providing that the translator was himself an adequate scholar and was aware without condescension that much subtlety must necessarily be lost in the translated script. This is a comparative matter. Thucydides and Herodotus and Plato can come across in a truly recognizable form, Greek poetry not so successfully but still importantly. Would one be better off by not reading Tolstoy, Dostoyevsky, and Goethe because one does not know Russian and German? The value and importance of translation and the access to a larger public than the professional one clinched my respect for the trade I was beginning to practice. Chicago and the College there and finally the Committee on Social Thought were to do the rest. The game seemed very much worth the candle.

Ruth was very quick-witted, emotional and open, and also given to driving difficult situations still further and then histrionically disposing of them. I became aware of all sorts of personal problems between her and Mark, and I could see the needling thrust coming just before it happened. Mark drank a lot—perhaps too much. He always worked slowly, but it was at his own pace. He said so to me and I am inclined to believe him. Ruth continually suggested to him that his drinking was harming his work and that the slowness with which he worked was a defect rather than a habit special to him. She certainly did not realize that it did not help to criticize it. He was a very stubborn man, and resented that sort of suggestion about his behavior. For all that, when Ruth was at her best, she had a magnetism that seized his imagination and made him as happy as he could be made, and the pair of them were ready to see their setting and their friends and everything that happened with a gaiety which was very catching. It certainly caught me.

Over all this small circle that I came to know, including the Brunswicks—Austrians, some Americans, French, and Italians—psychoanalysis lay like a threatening cloud. They were nearly all analysts, except for some friends of Mark, who were musicians of some sort; they had all been analyzed (mostly by Freud) and kept coming back for more. This had gone on for years and many of them seemed fairly stuck. Mark himself had been in analysis for nine years until he gave it up as hopeless. From the point of view of an outsider like myself (and one should add a very young outsider) it certainly seemed as if Freud's personal quirks and indeed his entire personality had come to obtrude itself too much into the analyzing process. A prominent analyst told me three or four years afterward that he thought that Freud had fallen in love with Ruth, much to the damage of the professional work of both. Some years after our Viennese time together Mark and Ruth decided to divorce and told me of it. They clearly were vexed and hurt by the want of decisive comment on my part.

"Surely," said Mark, "you did enjoy being with the two of us and saw us as a real couple." It was a hard question to answer honestly. Because although they did fascinate me as a couple, there was palpable discomfort exuding from them when they were together. Sometimes a couple disagrees and bitches at one another but it is possible to see that the internecine feuding, so upsetting to an onlooker, is bred of the vitality of the relationship itself and some quirk of the interaction of the two involved. This was not so with Mark and Ruth. Mark certainly became a much more unified person when he got divorced. And of course found another woman, a gentle music-loving Russian mathematician, and married her to the happiness of both. Equally, of course, the abandonment of the analysis helped. Very sadly, Ruth did not live long after leaving Vienna and coming home to America.

Return to Dublin: Ria Mooney

When I came back from Vienna, I assumed that I was going to stay in Trinity teaching classics, following on my appointment as a lecturer before I left. That indeed was the intention of the College, too, which had generously sanctioned my going away to learn German and study how classics was taught in Continental countries. Now there was to begin my real professional life, to last, probably, in Trinity for the rest of my time, like so many of the Fellows and professors. I cannot say that I was other than contented. The outlines had a reassuring feeling of ordinariness and I had always enjoyed myself there as a student, and if things had become a little duller and somewhat empty during the year after I had finished my Honors degree, I was eager now to apply what I had learned in Vienna about classical philology, and about how the German system, of which the Austrian was a part, thought students should be instructed.

What actually happened was a period of six months which changed everything so much that none of this previous design stayed in place at all. I had a very important love affair, and also a chance of getting to America and starting my teaching life there. I never came back to Trinity after that, and to Ireland only in a new form of contact, in which

I farm there roughly half the year and teach in Chicago the rest of it.

Let me say to start with: the theater had always been the art form that meant the most to me. The power of the individual voice and body to be itself but also artistically to be something other and universal, and of using the personal to be that other, has had a magic for me ever since I saw my first plays (other than pantomimes) at about the age of eleven. Nothing except the theater has had that power. Even in the related art form, the cinema, here and now there is a gap between what I see and any complete surrender to it. I watch the film but am hardly ever carried away into believing that this is an absolute truth such as I have never experienced in the world outside of the theater, which invariably is true when I see a great play well acted. This difficulty with films was intensified by my brief stay in Hollywood in 1937. It was there I first learned about the meaning of "rushes," and film-seeing has never been quite the same since.

Films are made out of short sections of acting cut up by the director and played over and over again for him until he is satisfied that the single sentences, phrases, or words have met his standard of perfection. Then the "rush" is stitched back to the last piece that has attained the same degree of satisfactoriness. But an actor, in live theater, invariably shows something, something very tiny, of the pull between the direct personality of his or her voice and gestures and the transformation that has been effected in them. This must be as good a transformation as the actor can make it from moment to moment, since, for that performance anyway, there is no second chance of mechanically erasing the word or the gesture which failed to make contact with the audience, that anonymous but conscious background which hovers at all levels of intensity, from extreme interest almost to disregard, in the actor's mind. The actor, man or woman, must bend all that is personal in voice, gesture, and movement to create a character that is not his or hers but one imaginatively grasped from an author's script. Then again that character lives inside a scheme of reality which must also come through to the audience. The tiny flaw, the momentary failure, is the guarantor of the genuineness of the histrionic art. We must get a bare glimpse of the struggle in order to grasp the dimension that acting brings to the play. It is a human act of creation of something not essentially human, except in image. This is why to see a great actor, man or woman, in a succession of different roles of quite different kinds of appeal over a limited space of time—weeks, months, or even years—as the old repertory companies used to allow their audiences to do, defines one's sensibility to the range of the art. The greats that shaped my own sense of theater, as I look back on them, command a special kind of reverence for me. John Gielgud, Laurence Olivier, Peggy Ashcroft, Siobhan McKenna and Maggie Smith, F. J. McCormick and Barry Fitzgerald, Sara Allgood and Ria Mooney, Derck Jacobi, Nick Pennell and Nick Rudall have each given his or her own imprint on the plays I have loved.

There is no substitute for performance observed, if you want really to enjoy theater in depth. But great performances open the mind to how the living voice, at least if one reads the play aloud at crucial places, can do something to convey to students some notion of how the written play comes to its proper life. This is especially true of poetic drama.

As I have said, I have always had some understanding of this since I was very young, and of course then only partially. But within a week of my return from Vienna I fell in love with an actress whom I had seen play a number of roles when I was still a student in school and college, though I had never known her personally. This affair, engaged in with all the attributes of love in one's early twenties, had a special and literally dramatic overtone. For some reason that I have never discovered since, both of us, a day or two before Christmas 1935, attended a performance of J. M. Barrie's *Peter Pan*. It was put on in the old Empire Theatre, long since demolished. Both of us were alone, and at the interval both of us went into the bar, when I said (the inevitable) "You are Ria Mooney aren't you? I have enjoyed seeing you play so often." We were launched. We talked plays for an hour without going back to *Peter Pan*. She had recently returned from the United States, where she had been playing mostly in the company of Eva Le Gallienne for a number of years. She had played her first roles in the Abbey when she was just a teenager. She admired Le Gallienne but in the end she did not want to go on playing in America. She wanted to come back to Dublin.

I have never seen a more dedicated actress. Every moment of emotion, surrender, rejection, or distress apparently stored itself in her mind, from which it emerged in wanted histrionic form. I became accustomed to seeing the transformation of the private passion, surely spontaneous and uniquely hers, into the superbly correct tone of voice or gesture harnessed to a fictitious person in a fictitious plot. *Not,* most emphatically, a swapping of her own personality with the play's role; very far from it. It was exactly the intensity and genuineness of the original experience transformed for an explicit purpose, but so transformed neither exactly by conscious intention nor by recollection, but by some awakening of the "real" or historic act into something evocative, transient, and vaguely aimed at eternity.

All this has been noticed many times, not least in *Hamlet* ("What's Hecuba to him or he to Hecuba, that he should weep for her?"). I can only say that it became something of a personal revelation to me. I did not confuse myself by wondering which was the "real" woman or think about nonsense like mimicry. But I knew that I was seeing for a short time someone for whose work, indissoluble from herself, I felt an utter and bewildered admiration.

I saw Ria in a lot of plays, counting those I saw before I knew her. I have seen her as Pegeen Mike in *Playboy of the Western World*; I have also seen her play the Widow Quin in the same play; I have seen her as Katie Roche in a little known but remarkable play by Teresa Deevy; I have seen her as Victoria Regina, in the play of that name. These were very disparate roles in performances at both the Gate Theatre and the Abbey in Dublin, and once or twice in London. Rather to my surprise she found something useful and even at times compelling in the way in which I entered into the performance of her parts: how I could see the details shaping themselves into strength or the reverse. I now know that this is a sort of minor gift I have—I think it might more honestly be called a facility for suggestion—providing the play has provocative meaning for me, and the actor (man or woman) is groping, with a clue, but with that clue startlingly emphasized by what I can see.

She was a very great actor. I am glad that some photographs taken of her for public presentation still keep before me in sharp relief the strength and hardness of the face in its histrionic revelation.

Inevitably the affair lasted only a very short time, and inevitably I was replaced by a real director. I felt the loss acutely, but without real surprise or resentment. I had known it could not last. The love affair had always the very stuff of the theater in it. It had a lasting effect in permeating my understanding of the theater and what I saw in it, which has had great influence on my classes on dramatic authors.

In the last part of her life Ria was director of the Abbey's junior theater, where the future company is trained. She was apparently a tremendous success at this. She died of cancer of the throat, thirty years ago.

America

How I got to America at all was one of those flimsy opportunities that could so easily not have happened. I left Vienna
in December 1935, and after teaching at Trinity for a term
decided to go to Greece in the summer of 1936, stopping in
Vienna again for a visit to the Brunswicks—which I felt sure
would be the last seeing of them in the Hasenauerstrasse.
In late June, Ruth's father Julian Mack, a very distinguished
judge of the Circuit Court of Appeals in New York, came over
to celebrate his seventieth birthday in Vienna. I was asked to
the party by the Brunswicks.

Julian was another of the very extraordinary Americans
who were to make me feel that I was among people such as
I had never met before. Certainly not as a breed or a class.
Julian's father had been a tailor and emigrated to Chicago
in the late nineteenth century. Julian grew up and took a
brilliant law degree at the University of Chicago in the early
1900s and eventually became a professor there. Privately, he
also amassed a quite considerable fortune. He was afterward
appointed to a federal board and became a trustee of Harvard
as well. His connection with his old university—Chicago—
also remained very close. Had his age suited the moments of
vacancy in the Supreme Court, the general feeling I gathered

was that he would have been chosen as a judge in the Court. He was a most impressive man at seventy, alive to anything or any person he found new or exciting. Of great dignity and decision of judgment, there was no pomposity in him. He also had most lovable absurdities. If you told Julian you were going somewhere in the city he knew better than you did, he would discuss with you for half an hour all the possible ways you could reach your destination. In such matters he was the very parody of a lawyer, without having any notion of it. I suffered more from this in New York later. If I rashly admitted that I was going from his hotel on the edge of Greenwich Village—the Fifth Avenue Hotel—to the Plaza at 59th Street, he would answer, "Wait a minute. You could of course travel straight there by the Fifth Avenue bus. But you could take the subway at 13th Street and get an express at 42nd and then a slow train to 59th. Or if you want to see something you haven't seen yet, you can go to Third Avenue and take a bus there, and then at 59th walk over to the Plaza . . ."

Julian had been told by president James Conant of Harvard to look out for bright young academics in his visit to Europe. Conant himself had aimed at getting the very cleverest young students to Harvard by a massive system of tuition exemptions and grants, all disregarding race, class, and background. He felt, I think, that Harvard's complacency and stuffiness needed to be shaken up, and he cordially believed that this was the way to do it. He certainly brought excellent students there who would never have got there otherwise, as my own one year's teaching at Harvard convinced me. But the relief from the complacency was something else, and I personally had no conviction that this was more than marginally punctured. In all my time in America, Harvard has been, to me at least, stuffy, unauthentically American, and quite dull.

Julian and I had a number of interesting conversations in Vienna, spontaneously occurring and with almost no inhibition on my side. I can only attribute this to Julian's tremendous humanity and modesty. He decided I might just qualify for Conant's interest. The Harvard classical people contacted my professors in Trinity, and the upshot was that I was offered a full-time tutorship and a part-time instructorship at Harvard, with a vague suggestion that I might go on to do graduate work there toward a Ph.D., and after that stay on in the American academic scene. It was a very generous offer, the second time I had been given something like it, the first one being the lectureship in Trinity—and I was still only twenty-three. I was, as I see it now, appallingly brash; not exactly impudent, for I did not see these things as coming my way out of merit. I was entirely aware of the degree of pure luck and chance in them. But brash in that I had no notion of how rare and unlikely such opportunities were. I was, honestly enough, trying to find out what I was good for, and what I liked doing. I was landed in classics, and I had no doubt about my interest in classical literature. But I had considerable doubt about teaching as a career. And with a naïveté hard not to resent in retrospect, I assumed that it was natural that I should be given the choice of picking a career and having great men treat me (even with amuse-ment) as a kind of equal, allowing me to play with my destiny with kindly help from them. This was America's amazing gift to me. There was Julian and his immensely important friends, like the two judges Learned and Gus Hand. There were in Cambridge Felix Frankfurter and his wife Marion, and Henry and Mary Hart. Thanks to these people, I learned to aspire to a kind of work that had never before taken any shape for me; and all of these people seemed to like to get to know me.

After all the years in between, this my beginning sentiment of admiration and awe about America has never entirely faded. It is in so many ways a deeply traditional country, where the re-spect for the Constitution, and a simplified but still largely correct understanding of it, extends from the greatest judges to the im-migrant of more than a few years' standing. But it has developed very few accretions of the ordinary class or social sort such as pervaded British, Irish, and most continental societies of which I know anything. The charge usually made is that America has substituted money for such psychological values. To an extent this is true. No president in America has yet become so without a

great fortune either inherited or of his own achievement behind
him. Nor has he attained the presidency without a huge amount of
money backing him. But in my time he has come from *anywhere* as
far as background goes. The uniformity of British prime ministers
and cabinet ministers in point of schooling, university training,
and above all genuine sophistication, is something entirely missing in their U.S. counterparts. But this fact about origin makes
ordinary people of America aware of democracy in a very special
way. They do not think that the president is intrinsically different
from themselves. It is just the appalling responsibility and size
of the office that separates them, and ordinary people in America
realize at least partly the problems and terrors of that kind of
responsibility. When president, he is far more than a politician.
He is both king as representative of all his people and chief executive. From FDR to Truman to Reagan to Clinton by an amazing
series of good luck chances—that one hopes cannot be just good
luck—men of the most diverse political beliefs and backgrounds
have transcended them to become leaders and representatives of
all Americans.

All of this is political comment on the United States by someone
not born there. It is, I fear, in its expression quite conventional
but it also belongs to my purely personal sense of America. It is
not only that I came to know, even if superficially, some of the
principal judges and political lawyers in the United States in 1936
and 1937. This was an immense gift given to a very young man
only, I think, because he was at least sensitive enough to know
how big the people were. And I also came to Chicago when the
University of Chicago was still newly under the direction of a very
great educator, Robert Maynard Hutchins, and his experiment
in general education. Nowhere on earth, it seems to me now,
could I have found myself in a setting where the fundamentals
of university education were being so seriously considered and
tested with a freedom of judgment and indifference to everything
but honest examination and argument. I was only an instructor,
but in the College of the late thirties and early forties rank counted
for almost nothing at all. Argument and the capacity to fight your

case and freely give and take the consequence was everything. I had never seen anything like this in my life.

And again, in 1940 I managed to buy a farm in Lemont about forty miles from the university and farmed it as best I could while driving into Chicago four days a week to teach. I did not know then, but I do now, that I was seeing the last, most expressive version of the Midwestern farm of the late nineteenth and early twentieth centuries. Mine was only 80 acres, but most of my neighbors had similar holdings up to 220 acres. In origin they were largely German but also Polish and Lithuanian, and usually second- and third-generation Americans. I lacked many of the gifts they had grown up with as American farmers. They were all creditable carpenters and not bad mechanics. I was neither of these. I did have a sense of livestock, and they recognized that.

But in all three of the areas into which I seemed to have merely stumbled—the political and legal, which were confined mostly to that year in Harvard with visits to New York and Washington, the far more important academic experience in Chicago in the years that followed directly, and finally in the ownership of the first farm that was ever mine—America had given me something that is unique. A sense of being estimated and actually earning something entirely one's own, on which one was judged and on which one acted. It was the way you went about your task, the way you made people feel that you *were*, the ruthless disengagement from anything superficial to the you that was yourself, that counted. I had never before and, I believe, have never again been challenged in such a way, and enjoyed the challenge with so much happiness and glee.

I keep getting echoes of those days even in the last few years. People like James Watson, the DNA researcher who declared that I made him understand Sophocles and Shakespeare; Dave Rubinfine, the great psychoanalyst; Mike Nichols and Elaine May, who studied with me now and then and who played my translations of the Greek plays; the classical scholars Allan Bloom and Seth Benardete. Across the years many of them have spoken for the truth of our first joint experience of many great literary works, that I had made with my understanding of drama a sense of excitement *and* truth for them and that they still, with all the changes of the forty or fifty succeeding years, found the truth that they had understood a valid one. I have never had so deep a certainty about the usefulness and achievement that my teaching could conceivably bring.

The directness of communication in the United States between people mostly unlikely to speak with one another elsewhere where I have lived astonished me, and again emphasized the importance of the commonness of their humanity. In the summer of 1937 my friend Henry Hart of Harvard Law School and his wife Mary offered to make me their companion in their annual drive across the country from Cambridge, Massachusetts, to the state of Washington, which was home to both of them. Henry had been asked to lecture in the law school in Berkeley. So they drove me from Cambridge to San Francisco, and this was another of those shattering American experiences. Not only the extraordinary extent of the country and its variety impressed me, but what D. H. Lawrence correctly described as its primitivism. The Cook City–Red Lodge highway through the Rocky Mountains makes one imagine what a countryside is like that is totally without man, something that is very hard to find almost anywhere in Europe. I lived in Berkeley most of that summer and saw a bit of the university there, but there was also an episode that particularly taught me something about America. While I was in Cambridge, Felix Frankfurter had introduced me to Sam Behrman, who was writing a play called *Amphitrion '37,* based on a French play which was itself based on the Latin of Plautus. In Behrman's hands it was only partly derivative and in general could fairly be described as a new play, but Berry was bent on knowing its antecedents, and he didn't read Latin and knew very little French. So he took me on to help with that and also to help with the actors Alfred Lunt and Lynn Fontanne, who were making difficulties in the Boston performances, which were indeed in a constant state of flux as Berry altered the text from night to night. I was told to see the play over and over again and convince Lynn particularly that in its newest form it suited her admirably and in fact found for the first time the most correct and most interesting version of the original, as she played various changes in her own inimitable way. It was very easy for me to be convinced of this myself, and she naturally thought very highly of my capacity as a critic. The end of it all was that Berry said that if I could get to Los Angeles later in the summer he would take me to the play's first night and also show me the sights of Hollywood.

Then began for a week or a week and a half the climax of my absurd transformation under the influence of the American scene in 1937. I went down to L.A., and not only was I taken to the premier of *Amphitrion '37* in a car with Hollywood stars but was taken to a party where I met Harpo Marx, that one of the three Marx brothers who always played as dumb. Now Felix Frankfurter had given me a special letter, in case I met Harpo in Hollywood, declaring to him how much his performances meant to him (Felix). Remember, this was 1937 and Frankfurter was still the public champion of the New Deal in America. He was to be within a year or two the Roosevelt appointment to the Supreme Court. He was also a Jew, as Harpo was, and, like the Marxes, someone who came to the United States in the early nineteen-hundreds and gained a universe which they could hardly have imagined in their youth. When I met Harpo I gave him Felix's letter. He went around the party all evening showing it and saying, "Do you know what I have here? A letter from Felix Frankfurter saying that he really enjoys what we are doing." I can't say how much the whole thing moved and impressed me. Another day Harpo took me to a prize fight and here to my amazement I saw him mimic directly all the expressions on the faces of both combatants. There was something peculiarly revelatory about this for the nature of clowning. He also took me to a dinner with Sam Goldwyn and Marc Connelly (playwright of *Green Pastures*). Goldwyn did not produce any of his famous absurdities for the occasion—does anyone ever, I wonder? Except for being dazed by the size of the bill at the Kakouk—it was two hundred dollars—I found that a rather ordinary sort of most unlooked-for occasion, with people one never expected to meet.

All of this in the first year and a half in America: the genuine if slight relation to Julian, Felix and their great lawyer friends, and the trip across the country and then the dream world of Hollywood constituted a kind of extravaganza on what America could be for me. But when I took the train, the old *Challenger*, which carried me in two days and three nights from San Francisco to Chicago in September 1937, I met, and I am proud to say did recognize right off, the solid place where I thought I could become someone decently and yet excitingly useful in my own right in a completely new way.

12

University of Chicago

When I came to find Harvard thoroughly disappointing—
something that was clear to me three months after I arrived
there in September 1936—I was going to go back to my job in
Trinity without any regret when, again, Julian Mack made
a contribution to my life. He said, "Harvard isn't America,
you know. Also, Harvard isn't American education either.
What is happening in Chicago now seems to me much more
interesting. If you like I'll write Hutchins and see if he has
anything he could give you." I had heard a little about the
Chicago academic revolution, though not nearly precisely
enough. However, I had enjoyed some aspects of America
very much and certainly had a tremendous regard for some
of the people I had gotten to know, and I said to Julian that
I would be very obliged to him if he would write Hutchins.
A week or so later Julian wrote me enclosing a single page of
note paper on which was written

> Dear Julian:
> I am sending a dean
> to see Mr. Grene.
>
> As ever,
> Bob

Somehow the absurdity of this prejudiced me strongly in the writer's favor. A university president who would write like that, even to an old friend, but a friend who was a most respected federal judge, must be something special—and likable. In the course of a month Richard McKeon was in New York and interviewed me. As I had been thinking about how to teach classical literature ever since I got the Trinity appointment and had been part of the courses which Radermacher gave in Vienna, some rather important aspects of the matter had become clearer. First, in a world where there was evidently less teaching of classics in the universities and the schools, and where the huge expenditure of time on the two languages which had been expected from the student was not going to be allowed for more than a few years from then, the old sort of philological training simply could not be the only one practiced. Besides, during my student years I had begun to wonder why we were never really asked to think seriously about what our Greek and Latin authors said to us—whether they were right or wrong, whether we enjoyed the poetry, whether we thought the history interesting or truthful, *why* in fact we were almost never required to know the meaning of what we read but only the form in which it was written.

Ideally one should be able to teach the language adequately and at the same time discuss the contents of the books as one would books written in English and other modern languages. But this proved very difficult, because the two ancient languages (and I knew that ideally we ought to be learning Hebrew as well) cannot be generally learned to the level that I had known myself to have attained at the end of my undergraduate career. After all, I had started Latin at nine and Greek at ten in school. It must be said that much of the elementary knowledge of ancient languages can be much more expeditiously and sensibly obtained by work when the student is more mature. But there is a limit to this. So I thought that what one was bound to do were two things simultaneously. Students who were going to specialize in modern languages and literature ought during their undergraduate career to read much of the classics in translation, and their teacher should teach Plato as a part of European philosophy, and Herodotus and Thucydides as part of Western history, and so on. Then the students who were specializing in classics should be taught Greek and Latin as well and as completely as their teacher could manage, but probably one half of even this work would have to be done in translation, the teaching itself being much like that which would be done for authors within broad divisions such as philosophy, history, and drama. I was prepared to hear that this was a betrayal of true classical study and education, but I thought that this objection was very specious, and indeed if one could not make some such deal for classics in modern university education, we might as well fold our tents and depart.

I talked to McKeon in this strain and he decided that I was the kind of man whom the new program in Chicago needed. When I got there, this seemed largely true. The way in which the undergraduate school was arranged was, in humanities and social sciences, very much along the lines I had sketched as those I wanted to follow. The end of the thing was that I was offered a job as lecturer in the Division of Humanities, which meant that I could list any course I liked in any department of the division (though, as I was to find, whether there would be any students for these unauthorized forays into higher learning was another problem altogether). The Classics Department viewed me with extreme suspicion as a dangerous import with Hutchins's connivance and undoubtedly opposed to the older order of the University of Chicago, which he was allegedly determined to destroy.

To win exams on classical texts mostly on philological grounds was something respectable, but it told me little about what I could do as a teacher. To teach those texts even to good students at Harvard who were interested in their literary, historical, or philosophical meanings was worthwhile and an advance on Trinity College. But to be thrown into the fascinating chaos of the University of Chicago at that time, when you met some of the brightest young students in the world, many of whom were New York and Chicago Jews, and all earnestly asking what Aeschylus' and Sophocles' plays meant—in the same way that they posed the question about the works of Shakespeare, Ibsen and Shaw (all of whom were also studied in the College, i.e., the undergraduate period)—all of this was a challenge to me as a teacher that I had not experienced before. I was also teaching Greek as a language, of course, and after one year at the university I knew that I had found a significance in teaching that language that I was very proud to have a share in.

The University of Chicago already had a record of doing new things in a new way when Robert M. Hutchins took over its management in 1929. I did not get there until 1937, when many of Hutchins's reforms had already been put into effect and some of the failures already admitted and dismissed. Therefore I can speak from personal knowledge only of the years from 1937 until the outbreak of the war, the skeletal war years themselves, and then the confused but intensely alive academic seasons from 1946 until Hutchins's departure in 1952, during which the returned veterans contributed tremendous vitality to the campus, and when the Committee on Social Thought (described below) was beginning to function as a proper independent entity. For the first two of these periods, I was mainly teaching in the undergraduate college and in the Greek Department; afterward in the Committee on Social Thought.

The University of Chicago had been founded in the eighteen-nineties by William Rainey Harper, who declared that he would staff it with the greatest professors that could be found for money. He offered salaries that no one had ever thought possible before; he made good choices also, and he succeeded in obtaining big money from the Rockefellers while skillfully avoiding committing himself to a straightforward Baptist university. He found a unique site in the grounds of the World's Fair, on the Midway, in the heart of South Chicago; the university still stands in a very substantial parkland of its own.

For some intervening years after the death of Harper, which occurred in 1906, the university had a quiet time until the appointment of Max Mason in 1926. Mason was president for only three years, when he left under some particular and undisclosed circumstances. Then the trustees took the monumental step of offering the position to Robert Maynard Hutchins.

Hutchins was one year older than the century. He had driven an ambulance in the First World War, and after getting his law degree at Yale, became dean of Yale Law School in 1926. From there he came to Chicago to take over the presidency when just thirty years old. He was a man who in his combination of talents would seem unlikely to have attained such important academic administrative posts so early in his life. He was certainly a great charmer—handsome, tall, and noble in movement and gesture. But also sharply and fiercely witty and most unwilling to suffer fools gladly. It is hard for me to be just in dealing with his education movement in the university. The ideas in it were so deeply right but sometimes too simplistic and sometimes too inflexible for application, except by someone of consummate political skill and therefore probably someone much older than thirty.

Briefly, he thought that the American university system had gone wrong in all sorts of ways, but notably in doing away with a fixed and general education for undergraduates in favor of Dr. Eliot's* permission to put together any number of any courses that happened to interest the young student. In his two wonderfully clever and amusing books, *The Higher Learning in America* and *No Friendly Voice*, Hutchins scarified American academia as offering courses in hotel management and dishwashing with no proper formal education at all (one must allow some element of caricature). Specialization between seventeen and twenty-one deprived the country as a whole, he thought, of an educated society which had learned the great truths that man at different times had entertained about freedom and organization, God and natural law, causation in history. In science, while not in the least neglecting the nuts and bolts of pragmatic science, he insisted on the importance of the general ideas on which such pragmatism was based.

*Charles William Eliot, a former president of Harvard University.

An undergraduate education according to Hutchins must be taught through original texts, not secondary books about the subject. Hobbes, Locke, Tom Paine, the Federalist Papers and Marx were what should be read in the social sciences. In humanities there were Shakespeare, Greek tragedy in translation, Tolstoy and Dostoyevsky, but also very prominently Plato, Aristotle, Aquinas, Descartes, Hume, Hegel, and Kant. The historical connections of these texts with one another or with other features of the times in which they appeared were almost ignored. It was axiomatic that every great book could be apprehended directly by anyone of proper intellectual gifts who would take it seriously and ask the basic questions of it. I still think this is the proper direction for undergraduate studies, and to a great degree for much of graduate study also. But it left a lot to be arranged in the matter of teaching and staffing.

Hutchins was also concerned about the way in which a student would qualify for his degree. He felt that the passing of courses to reach the needed number of credits was usually too dependent on the student's skillful work at satisfying the particular instructor, and that this killed independent judgment. He wanted some much more objective and more general tests for becoming a B.A. Unfortunately these also had a very simplistic side. The four segments of the College—humanities, social science, physical sciences, and biological sciences—were each to have one big exam at the end of every year, and passing all of these gave the student a B.A. Exams taken at the end of each quarter were only to let the student see how he was progressing; they did not count for the final result. But partly because of the immense job of reading such a huge amount of exam papers of the conventional written kind, and partly out of some misguided belief in objectivity, Hutchins allowed that the big exams were to involve almost no writing of any sort of individual essays. The questions were of the kind that proffered the examinee five possible alternative answers to choose from, with the result to be checked mechanically.

The Department of Education plumped unequivocally for such "objective examinations." They declared that recognition of the correct answer was the same thing as writing an essay to that effect. It is really hard to believe that anyone sensible ever thought of such a thing. The result was quite certainly a big decline in the writing skills of the students. Hutchins knew this disadvantage all right—but he tried to set against it a plan of his own for small student seminars, which unfortunately was never accepted.

So the Hutchins College rested on his plan of these four divisions, paralleling the four graduate divisions. It relied on a small number of lectures (one a week) and a number of discussion sections to meet three times a week, with twenty-five students each and an individual instructor. The lectures were supposed to open up the subject to be discussed; the instructors would then teach the involved books in their own way.

The graduate divisions were bitterly opposed to the whole concept. While they were prepared to accept a very moderate amount of general courses for undergraduates—a sort of rather vaguely organized history of Western civilization—they had fed their own specialties by small, particular courses which were compulsory for moving from undergraduate to graduate studies, and they had no desire to change this.

The Physical and Biological Sciences Divisions simply refused to accept the College course as qualifying students for graduate study in these fields, and they put themselves as an efficient roadblock to the further progress of those who had just passed through the Hutchins College. Either the undergraduates had to do the department's special courses over and above those specified in the College, or they were turned down for divisional graduate work at Chicago. Indeed, for many years the departments of mathematics and the sciences admitted hardly any students who had graduated from the Hutchins College. They all came from elsewhere.

The social sciences faculty were slightly easier to deal with. What they complained of in the Hutchins program was just the same as what irked the professors in the physical and biological sciences. They were doubtful as to the need for any general intellectual training; and they wanted their students to spend their undergraduate years studying the newer fields of anthropology, statistics, psychology, and sociology. Instead they found them reading about political theory in Plato, Aristotle, and Cicero, and history in Herodotus, Thucydides, and Tacitus. (These texts often figured in both social science and humanities courses in the College.) The Social Sciences Division could have done what physical and biological sciences had done and excluded them from admission to their graduate programs, but they did not; possibly because of the influence of Robert Redfield, the eminent and enlightened anthropologist in their midst.

We had other problems in humanities, which was my field. Richard McKeon, the Hutchins nominee who was dean of that division, was also put in charge of humanities in the College, along with a theologian, Clarence Faust. For some years there were serious discussions among the staff about the various books in the courses. But gradually McKeon and Faust began to manipulate these in the direction of a doctrine of their own—the famous Chicago School of Criticism. This was based on Aristotle's *Poetics*, which was taken as the key not only to the Greek tragedies but also to Shakespeare and all other subsequent drama; and by almost incredible distortions, to English lyric poetry as well. Novels were only Greek epics reborn. Nothing in all Western literature after the Greeks needed new methods of explication.

There were ten or twelve of us, instructors and professors, all teaching the same books to our discussion sections, and it was held that this necessitated the establishment of some common position on the books. There was no merit at all—in fact the reverse—in having differing views of each book explained to the students. David Daiches (the Scottish literary critic) and I were the sole, but very vocal, heretics. David went back to do Intelligence work for the British in 1942, but he was already slated for removal from the College staff. I soldiered on for a couple of years more, and got my dismissal notice from the College in 1945. Only two dissident statements did anything to mitigate the bitterness of this slur on my professional career. One was that Faust informed the administration that he had no fault to find with my knowledge of teaching per se; I was simply an impossible person to have in a course which ought to present an agreed point of view on a literary work and the terms in which it was considered. This at least put the matter in its proper light, if that is what you want to do with a course in literature. The second was that Ronald Crane and Elder Olson, both prominent members of the staff and strong supporters of the School, openly disagreed with the verdict on me and stated that they had frequently disagreed with me, "as gentlemen might," but that that was no reason for dropping me.

However, McKeon had decided to remove me not only from the College but from classics, too. I spoke to Hutchins, who told me, fascinatingly, that in my first term in Chicago he had put a note in my file: "This man is not to be fired without consulting me." The note is still in the records to be read; and McKeon and Faust had not consulted him.

Hutchins then asked me to join the newly formed Committee on Social Thought. This was his own creation, along with the economic historian John Nef, who was its first chairman, the anthropologist Robert Redfield, and the economist Frank Knight. The other members were young men who, like myself, had had trouble with their conventional professional departments: the sociologist Edward Shils, the art historian Otto von Simson, and the Thomist philosopher Yves Simon. The idea was that the teaching members of the Committee should be specialists of a high order in particular subjects, but that we all distrusted a strictly technical specialization in the education of our students.

It is a graduate program, designed to deal with studies in humanities and social science, with aspirations toward Ph.D.'s of a "larger" character than the average. We are committed to very high standards in the students we admit, give our own degrees, rely heavily on tutorials, and allow our students the run of the university for any courses that they want to take, in or out of the Committee. The first three years of their work with us are devoted especially to about a dozen significant texts in philosophy, history, and "imaginative literature" from ancient, medieval and modern times, with the particular books chosen by the student with approval by the faculty. He or she will turn in papers on

David with a student, at the end of a class, c. 1993

these from time to time, and finally take an exam in the course of a week consisting of essays in response to questions set by the faculty relevant to these "fundamental texts"; and if this is satisfactory, will go on to work on a Ph.D. in a special area of interest. The Committee was from the beginning very idealistic as to our intellectual objectives; and it still is. I also think that it makes a very fair shot at teaching in the light of this idealism; and that there is some common mark on most of our students, and not a bad one, by the time they finish. I am very proud of the quality of the people that we have turned out, and of the work that they have gone on to do.

I have now been associated with the Committee for close to fifty years, and it is the only educational institution that I know small enough to be able to live by its principles. I am sure there are Oxford or Cambridge colleges which do so, but it is a very rare thing in America, Ireland, or the few European universities I know

David Grene in his office at the University of Chicago, c. 1985

anything about. As a rule, universities will be constantly challenging their departments about the numbers of students they admit, whether the faculty they want to appoint have enough publications to their credit, and so on. Thanks to our size and oddity, we have remained blessedly free from this, to pursue our own choices.

Regarding Hutchins and his leadership, he was a man of exceptional bravery and determination. During the McCarthy era when everyone's job was on the line, he defended our university against the Broyles Commission of Illinois, which wanted to comb through the political activities of our teaching staff and decide who should be fired as communists. Also when the millionaire Charles Walgreen attacked Hutchins for having a history department where his own niece was taught Marxism, Hutchins, with his natural bonhomie, induced Walgreen to endow a series of lectures on democratic institutions. "I am delighted to have all controversial subjects debated in the university," he said, "but I will not have any of them dropped or discriminated against except on strictly intellectual grounds."

In addition to the resentment that Hutchins aroused in some of the senior faculty by the programs that he initiated in the College, however, there were other points, some ideological and some practical, which led to conflict. One was that he thought there was a right and a wrong way to think about the questions that the Western world had repeatedly set itself, from the classical age to the twentieth century. He despised the relativism of those who talked of the difference in how philosophic problems *looked* at different historical moments. He had very strong feelings about his favorite literary texts, but perhaps too often because the author's vision in the poem, play or novel seemed to affirm his own. He had less of a gift for admiring the size and power of a vision with which he ultimately disagreed. He had almost none for letting the truth or untruth, as it appeared to him, live in some limbo of nondecision until time and experience crystalized his final judgment. His belief in logic and his lawyer's skill at elucidating it very often proved a disadvantage. It undermined the latent ambiguities in his mind, which were richer than the brilliance of his direct conclusions and their expression.

Mortimer Adler was a professor whom Hutchins had adopted out of Columbia University. He and Hutchins gave courses together on "Great Books," where Hutchins did most of the epigrammaking and much of the jibing, and Adler did the missionary work, where reason and logic invariably showed what was right—and permanently right. This caused a lot of flak on campus about Hutchins's dictatorial ways of forcing the acceptance of his ideas.

At one point Hutchins made an announcement that promotion in the College should be for either teaching or research (of course for both when that was possible), and in fact it was to be recognized that the staff of the undergraduate College would be more often teachers than researchers. This theory of the division of teaching and writing seems to me nearly always an unlucky one. Everybody who has taught for a long time knows that some great scholars cannot—God knows why—write. Unfortunately they often also cannot teach, but their knowledge and the spiritual depth of their search for it entitles them to a place in the university, which they invariably enrich. But outside of these rare people, most of those who teach want at times to reach a bigger audience than the intimacy of their special pupils. It certainly seems true, though curious, that when you try, as Hutchins did, to arrange for teaching and writing academically to be each similarly rewarded, you do avoid having the staff produce books, bad or good; but you also get most of your teaching done without freshness or originality. The simply histrionic part of the communication seduces some of the teaching staff. These probably do little harm but not much good. Far more of them settle for simply general statements about their authors or their positions which they formulated years ago and trot out repeatedly because they have long ago given up rereading their texts with any freshness of approach. Their job, as they see it, is *just* teaching, and they are usually complacent enough to think that they have learned the "right" answers to most of the questions raised about the writers they are reading. Such teachers offer no stimulus to students and no new life to the books they are reading with them.

Hutchins also proposed that there should be only one title in the university—"member of the teaching staff"—and salaries would be adjustable in terms of need (for family, etc.) rather than on the existing system of rank. Thus a needy and married instructor could, by the decision of a university committee appointed for the examination of such cases, come out earning more than a celibate or wealthy full professor. The professors were not pleased. This was never enacted, but he did put through a plan under which every faculty member was paid what was regarded as a reasonable full-time salary for his position; and anything additional which he earned by publications or outside lectures became the property of the university. Another highly unpopular move (reversed after Hutchins's departure).

In 1948 and 1949 Hutchins had formidable rows with the teaching staff, and the senior faculty of the university finally presented the trustees with a memorandum characterizing his administration as dictatorial and directed against the proper faculty participation in the government of the university. But his intense idealism, and his courage in pushing the reforms that he believed in, had generated tremendous enthusiasm and loyalty among the junior faculty; and within days the junior staff (including myself) sent another memorandum to the trustees expressing total disagreement. We cited what Hutchins had done for the staff in the matter of the Broyles Commission: how he refused to allow the state legislators to come to our private university and "investigate" us on the charge of communism; the hundred and one ways he had defended us against slanders by the state, the city, the media; how he had overcome his own repugnance to the atom bomb project so as to allow it to proceed within the university, because he felt it his patriotic duty to do so. These, we said, were very far from the acts of a dictator, nor did they show sympathy with what dictatorship had come to mean in our time. I am very glad to say that we received an entirely generous and sympathetic answer from the trustees, and the senior faculty's attack was received with a cold acknowledgment coupled with some doubts about the accuracy or relevance of its main evidence.

But Hutchins was very hurt by the whole episode and he began to think of leaving. I saw him upon my return from a six-month sabbatical in Europe in 1950-51 when the news of his resignation was already public. I asked him why he had done it, and he said, "There is really nothing I can bring to fulfillment here anymore. I

David with one of his children, Chicago, 1966. Photo by James Stricklin.

have raised opposition all around. If I stay on, I am afraid that one day I will wake up to find myself the grand old man of the Midway. I don't want that." It is possible to find this comment of his frivolous. I don't. He passionately wanted to be *doing* something in which he believed. He had neither the patience nor, indeed, the insight to see when some of his previous plans were still leading to good results.

Hutchins had made an extraordinary contribution in the launching of a general program in literature and social science as the most significant aspect of undergraduate training. The present day College lives on in a form not really different from what he envisaged; and the program has been widely imitated throughout undergraduate education in the United States. There is also no doubt whatsoever that the basic assumption of his Chicago plan—that undergraduates should study great original texts instead of secondary redactions—took hold of the American undergraduate experience and has never let go. The modern wave of enthusiasm for other than Western texts may not be a blessing to education, but it certainly has a seriousness that the old potted commentaries dealing in vague, unsupported historical and philosophical positions did not. Finally, I will most sincerely claim that I have never seen better students and have never enjoyed teaching as much as in the College and in the Committee on Social Thought. These great contributions of Hutchins—the emphasis on original texts, and the encouragement of independent-mindedness of the students, and the freshness and vigor of the atmosphere at its best—were indeed invaluable and they were undeniably and characteristically his.

I am very proud of our last interchange. I wrote a little book of essays, *Reality and the Heroic Pattern,* more than twenty-five years ago now. The essays dealt with the last plays of Sophocles, Shakespeare, and Ibsen. I dedicated it to R. M. Hutchins and the university "which he did so much to build" and sent him a copy. I got an answer, a couple of lines as his letters so often were: "What you have to say or to write always stirs my thoughts to life."

_13_

Farming

In the twentieth century, my interest in farming and Greek and Latin literature hardly seemed likely to be tracks which would have many followers or even engage much interest. Small farming, we are continually told, is in decline, and personal farming, which is the only kind I care about, is generally small farming. Classical literature, once so important in education, has been largely superseded both by training of a more technical sort, for those who think of education solely in terms of preparing to make a living, and by the host of more modern branches of learning like psychology, sociology, and so on that seem more pertinent to the existing world. I do not think that either of these trends, so regularly and so glibly presented, is quite as true as it pretends to be. The continent of Europe is still mainly characterized by small farms—by farms of less than a hundred acres. In the United States, where farms are much bigger, the overwhelming proportion is still family farms. And though it is true that classics has been pushed rather into the background in education, there is a strong feeling in most sophisticated circles everywhere that the beginnings of our civilization and its recovery in the Renaissance ought to be part of modern man's knowledge. Above all, as I see it, the way of life for individuals and knowledge that supports that way of life lie open now to choice—far more than they ever did in the past when, till a very short time ago, such choosing was the privilege of aristocrats or very rich people. I am convinced myself that the main excellence of modern life is its capacity to allow choice in the creation of crevices into which one can move and live at some depth. To do so, one must abandon the idea that one's earnings must be the top amount possible to obtain. Crevices are rarely as richly endowed as that. Whether you will affect many other people or only a few seems to me almost a matter of chance; but with a decent share of self-respect and some solid personal tastes and the capacity to enjoy them, one can be fulfilled and happy. At least, one does not find oneself constantly mouthing second-hand sentiments caught from other people's lips. I can say honestly that I have found quite a lot of farmers both here and in Ireland, and here and there in my short travels elsewhere, who have just this sort of life and feel this sort of values. And in university education, if one can turn one's attention from the arid professionalism which afflicts, most unfortunately, the study of literature in universities, the emphasis on method and categorization of art, and the silly rat race of promotion, depending on too early and too frequent publication, there is a real thrill in the deepening of one's knowledge and understanding, and, almost miraculously, in sharing it with a substantial minority of students and colleagues.

This matter of choice has grown in the context of a shrinking of the automatic inheritance of land and the disappearance of a nearly automatic version of education. Some farmers still become farmers because they have almost no other prospect of making a living. This is certainly the case in a country like India. Some farmers, a tiny but vocal minority, farm because they believe, quite falsely I think, that they can make more money that way than any other. They always try to own very big farms and for the most part, during my lifetime, have gone broke. Some farmers still inherit their farms from their fathers or more often less directly from an uncle, cousin, or more distant relative, and such farmers, having been given what is in effect a large slice of capital, stick with it largely out of inertia. But there is a growing minority of farmers who become so purely through choice, and in some instances, having almost no prior knowledge of farming, somehow manage to get together enough money to start. Very often nowadays, such people combine farming with some other way of earning money. This is a great help, for farming demands capital to take care of necessary changes, and it is very hard indeed to supply that capital from the actual running of the place. This is what I have managed to do myself.

The small farm, the home in the country, the values of the rural life against those of the city—how often do these arguments recur within the last twenty years in a diversity of popular literature. And how laboriously have I myself tried to disentangle them! I wanted to think that a "place in the country" was something trivial in comparison with the "real" small farming that I wish so earnestly to see survive—but how peremptorily now I realize that this is not so. Inside of modern society the people who want to live in some functional relation to land and animals are my spiritual kinsfolk. They are not just voyeurs. They have mostly come to own at considerable expense a small acreage, and usually have to rehabilitate it to live there, as opposed to existing in their ordinary jobs in the city. I now recognize, as I did not earlier, the genuineness of their association with the land. It is not what is called in affectionately contemptuous terms "romantic"; it is a true and realistic revelation of land, animals, and birds, of rain and sunshine—and thunder and drought and floods—as matters that truly affect their lives, as part of the personal delights and hazards which drove them to own their "places."

This community of people I have known from a very few friends, but far more from a number of writers (mostly American) like Wendell Berry and Noel Perrin. Those people and those books matter deeply to me. They don't matter abstractly, as though they were part of an argument where I was on their side. They matter because they really feel, as I do, what farming means to us. This is complicated because I and these champions of modern country life are saying something very different from most of our contemporaries. About wanting to live within earshot of the sounds of the countryside and nothing else; about seeing and perhaps working land as man has done since infinite time; about knowing animals as a part of one's universe of understanding and discourse, as a powerful alternative to an exclusive concern with human ideas, aspirations, claims on one's social being.

But I belong—I probably cannot know entirely why—to the statistically slightly odder class which wants to be small farmers, either exclusively or as a sideline to the rest of what makes them a living. Small farming as an attractive job depends on the possession of a mind not now common. There must be a pleasure in association with animals, a manual skill and joy in handling them, and in the management of the little universe which is a small farm. In other cases there must be very much the same feeling about growing crops, and watching the life of plants that one has personally placed in the ground, as man has done for so much of his time on the planet Earth. The man or woman concerned must find in this work his or her fundamental satisfaction. This is a known phenomenon in some professions, as among doctors, engineers, or carpenters, where the most remarkable representatives drive themselves unmercifully at their work because it is there that they are most fulfilled intellectually and physically. Now farming does belong in this category, though it is rare to have that recognized. You had better face up to that fact if you want to be a small farmer, and you must recognize also that you had better be a devotee of the job itself, because society will not pay you a large salary, as it would for the exercise of what are called the professions.

To choose to be a small farmer implies some degree of intellectual discrimination and a willingness to disregard the attraction of being like most other people. There is an age-old prejudice against farming, as a life of hard work and no thinking. We are constantly being told that man "naturally" abandons working the land in

David milking a cow on his Irish farm

David feeding the ducks

favor of a more complicated and significant way of spending time. I suppose that there is some evidence in support of this kind of thinking from the past, though even then, I think, only when speaking of a farmer working a farm not his own. These have become very rare birds nowadays, with only a few people renting large or small farms and even fewer working steadily as hired farmhands (apart from seasonal fruit-pickers, etc.). Farming is now either a very large venture personally conducted by one or two persons, or a very small venture personally conducted. Large corporation farming except here and there in vegetable or fruit production is becoming as rare as the disappearing centralized farms of the communistic past. The delight of making and shaping a piece of land and its animal inhabitants, this peculiar kingdom, is uniquely satisfying to the human being with this appetite—because he can himself *do* nearly everything necessary. It is the very expression of himself. And yet there is also a disinterestedness in such farming. Some contradiction does exist between farming and the purely business side of making money.

It is summed up in the eighteenth-century folk saying "Farm as if to live forever, live as if to die tomorrow."

Perhaps anything that one cares enough about in modern society has to have an opposite to illustrate by contrast what it is that one likes. The principal foe to my feeling for the place in the country, small farm part-time farming, is the delight in the *maximization* of effort and achievement. It is particularly annoying in the agribusiness rhetoric directed toward the small farmers in a country like Ireland. "If you are making a small living from farming based on, say, twelve to fifteen cows, why don't you rise to be chiefs of your profession and have thirty?" It can be done—if you divide your grazing into acre strips with electric wire, if you buy replacement heifers instead of raising your own, if you farm with close attention to every new and "scientific" wrinkle in agricultural "discovery." In such a system there is no value to be placed in the moments of contemplated or indeed active happiness. The other day I had turned out a flock of sheep into a new pasture and a neighbor stopped, as he was driving by, looking at me standing watching them move into their new surroundings. He said, "You can see you really like the job." There is no need to have this point made explicitly in the media all the time. But it is of the essence of true farming now and I believe always has been. If you farm in such a way that these moments are replaced by gross comparisons of how many cows you have now and how few so many years ago, and how much money you are making now in comparison with what you were making then—give farming up. Apart from what such an outlook is doing to yourself—this perpetual marathon-testing—farming will never give satisfaction. Farming isn't a maximum money-maker in industrial society and never will be, because modern people will not pay as much money for food to put in their mouths as opposed to things they find more interesting than eating, or more self-satisfying in impressive social ways. In a way they are quite right. But someone has to produce the food that is elementarily necessary. Intrinsic to the production of food there is an impersonal joy.

FARMING IN LEMONT

From about the first moment that I was officially a university teacher, I have combined teaching with farming. The two are so interdependent in my mind, for the satisfaction of my existence, that I cannot, even now when I am old and can do so much less in farming, see a possibility of discarding one or the other.

By disposition I believe in holding on to every acre of land one has ever owned. My disposal of two of these farms corresponded with the pressures of various factors in my life that had nothing to do with farming as such, but with the imperative need to get rid of the particular farm I owned in favor of buying another somewhere else. The eighty-acre American farm in Lemont which I bought in 1940, as the first, was an extraordinary occasion of joy and excitement. Here I could combine my living on the farm and driving in to teach at the University of Chicago, and that for a very considerable period of time seemed the happiest way to live. Unfortunately, the very shortness of the distance separating the farm from the city proved its undoing. Within ten years of its possession, I found all the surrounding territory being developed for suburbs, the keeping of livestock banned, since the area was zoned for housing, and finally the value of the land increasing entirely out of line with what I could possibly make from it. At the same time some streak of ambiguity in myself kept urging me to think of retiring to Ireland for part of my time each year and doing my farming and teaching in separate stints. It seems absurd, but it has worked out better that way. Though it means that I must farm through half of the year and must necessarily live there, it is just possible to find hired men in Ireland to do the work when I am away and pay them out of the proceeds of a fifty-acre farm. You can't find hired farm labor in the United States except for "working managers" whose salaries could easily surpass the total profits of such a small farm. Also, by 1950 I was seeing the writing on the wall for my sort of small mixed farm in middle America, thanks to mechanization and, in my instance, the pressure of suburbanism. I knew that the small farm, in much the same form, has for the last eighty years or so survived in Ireland and the mechanization is still less than total; the urbanization of large stretches of countryside is nonexistent.

My American farm was the first land I had ever owned and the first house, and, as such, something infinitely precious. To other eyes than mine and occasionally to mine too it didn't look so attractive. The house stood on one side of a small road, the barn on the other, and the small road at that time (1940) ran unsurfaced between two major roads.

Winter in the Midwest in those days was always very severe. We got tremendous spells of snowfall and subzero weather. The farm's location fitted it to small farming in the nineteenth century, but hardly to accommodate someone in wintertime trying out modern transport (a small car) traveling thirty-five miles a day to his place of business. Also, unluckily, my farmhouse did not have central heating, since the basement had never been fully dug out. The heat in winter was furnished by a couple of giant stoves of the kind that I knew in Vienna—but in Vienna those heavy old nineteenth-century houses held in the heat much better than the nineteenth-century wood of which my Illinois farmhouse was built. The barn had grown dilapidated and not of the standard necessary to supply the market for liquid milk. You could ship cream if you took it daily to the local train in Lemont, but that was one chore too many when at least four days a week I had to make the trip to the university. There was a lot of reconstruction and repair necessary for both farm and house, and absolutely no spare cash to do it with. We bought that farm for $10,000 with a down payment of $2,500 to be made after three years. Till then we were renting it at $50 per month, but on the secure understanding that it could not be sold until three years were up and then only if we failed to provide the down payment. In fact, the man who owned it had long since left the state, and it was his brother who had to try to sell it. He had had no success for several years, and had been reduced to renting it. The financial stringency on both sides of this bargain was reflected in the agreement in which the former tenants, a French-Canadian family, were tenants by the month only, with no further security than thirty days. It is easy to imagine what sort of tenants they would be, and exactly what was the result of their farming.

Yet it was such a place and time that allowed me to see a wonderful series of events which I had never been part of in Ireland and which was to endure not very long in that part of America. In winter, for local transport we drove sledges in the snow. It was not until after my first three years that there was a snowplow that came down our little Derby Road. All those Christmas cards in Ireland, cheerful inanities with sledges, sleigh bells, and mounds of snow, sprang into an incredible reality. The communal struggle of me and my two or three neighbors to get to the outside world in the morning (my nearest neighbor, Tony Seiler, worked with the AT&SF Railroad) was both exciting and somehow fun. It is all so long ago—we were so young. I remember that Tony for a while used a very small *burning* lamp under the hood of the car to keep it warm. I remember another neighbor who hitched a mule to his car, pulled it the requisite fifty or a hundred yards, and when it started got out and released the mule, who trotted back to his open barn dragging the evener which had enabled him to pull the car. I remember hauling in cornstalks with the sledge, which was only the wagon converted with runners instead of wheels, when the cold was intense but the excitement of cantering with the sledge over the snow entirely overpowered the discomfort. Most of all, though to outsiders less dramatic, I remember how I learned to plow and work up land for crops. In Ireland on the farms of my Tipperary cousins there were scarcely any crops; it was all permanent pasture, as it still is on those farms, and as it is on my present small Cavan farm. It was America that taught me how to plow and sow and harvest corn and cereals; it was also America that taught me, as an ideal, to raise all the food for myself and my livestock. This sort of interlocked farming is now unfashionable, at least in the most fertile land in the Midwest, which specializes in just corn and soybeans. In my time there were always dairy cattle in addition to crops, or hogs or fattening cattle. The fixed support price for corn and the scarcity of extra help to take care of livestock have made this change; very much for the worse, in my opinion at least. It has led farmers with five to six hundred acres of land to put in crops and take them out again in two or three months and take outside jobs for the rest of the year. The loss in topsoil from this monoculture is appalling, and the pollution arising from insecticides and herbicides is now an acknowledged fact.

We started with something that might be described as subsistence farming with some supplementary cash attached. We had all our meat—not only chicken and ducks, but bacon and lamb and mutton and goat's meat—and we had milk and butter. But we also sold lambs from our flock of fifty or so ewes, kept goats and raised them, and fattened seventy or eighty pigs for sale a year. After a couple of years of "share labor" with neighboring farmers, which was dictated by my almost total want of agricultural machinery, I began to acquire three horses to do the field work and hauling, but also supplemented them later with one big old 10-20 tractor which came still with steel lugs instead of rubber tires. If you drove this on a surfaced road, you were naturally unpopular with the county council, so I avoided that. But for slogging along, towing two fourteen-inch plows and plowing five acres a day or disking ten to fifteen, it was splendid. This left a lot for horses to do, planting corn, cultivating corn, mowing, making and hauling hay—aside from drawing out the manure. It was a perfect solution, and such old-fashioned but powerful mechanization was very cheap in the early 1940s. One must also remember that we were now facing into four or five years of war, when all forms of fuel were hard to get and there was every reason to use horses when one could do so. This first farm of mine, the American one, was a splendid blend of mechanization and old-time farming. I really cannot see why a version of it could not actually have survived. What happened is something like this: At the end of the war, the factories which had during the war exclusively been busy producing machines for the army turned back to producing tractors. They decided that the market to attack first was the area still occupied by small farms. After all, the factories produced tractors for sale, and the farmers' horses were in direct competition for the provision of power. So from about 1947 to 1955 advertisements and personal agents worked at selling the tractor-cum-horses farmer a little light tractor, to supplement his heavy one, to do the corn planting, corn cultivation and hay work instead of the last team. These small tractors cost eight to ten times more than a team of horses and at least as much to keep up as a team. I do not really think that the team was supplanted on the grounds of economics. What did it in were two factors. First, as all farmers now had cars, there grew a sort of mental impatience with horses. You had to harness them in the morning and take them out of work for a midday feed, and you couldn't simply leave them in the field when you went for lunch; in all these respects convenience called you to notice that animal power, as against mechanization, was always a stupid leftover. Those of us who felt differently, and there were quite a few and by no means all older people, were assailed by a different sort of compulsion. The older horse machines were relatively cheap and simple. The agricultural machinery companies deliberately discontinued their production, replacing them with motorized models nearly all geared to the power takeoff of the tractor. It was clear that, as one's machinery gave out and as what was left of it that was not yet fit for the scrap heap would soon be so, one simply would have no tools left to use animal power. What was at work here was a vague inclination toward mechanization—a something in the air, a psychological element in one's fancy, and, added to this, the purposeful exploitation of the remaining opening for tractors by making it impossible to farm with horses at all.

The next step, which I didn't see at first hand in America because I ceased farming there and started up in Ireland, where more gradually the same thing happened, was to put on the market steadily more powerful tractors—much dearer, of course. These created an appetite for more and more land on each farm, since the new tractor enabled the farmer to work more land, and the cost of the extra mechanization caused him to buy or rent more. Gradually, the population of the farms fell off from 10 percent of the

population in 1950 to 2 percent in 1990; and it is now the boast
of agriculture in the United States and in many other countries
of the industrialized world that enough food is produced for a
nation's people by an absolute minimum of farmers.

In the modern climate of opinion, where there is a strong
undercurrent asserting the dullness and monotony of agriculture,
there are always many people who readily accept the industrial
idea that the less help needed, the better. It is perhaps worth
looking at the other side of the same proposition. It is, in most
countries, not a question of losing hired help from farms. Such
labor is very scarce in any part of the world, in view of the constant
appeals of the superiority of city life. What is happening is that
there are fewer and fewer farmers themselves, and those who
are left are forced to farm at a speed and a tension which leaves
any hardship of the past simply nowhere. Whatever intelligent
opposition to this endless expansion there was, was effectually
stifled, since the agricultural journals depend almost entirely for
their existence on large agribusiness concerns and these are the
firms that pay for the advertisements. Of course, if people want
to go to the cities and try to find work, no one is going to stop
them. If one looks at the hideousness of much of city life, the
unemployment, and the violence, one might just wonder. There
has been almost no forum in which abstract questions could be
raised about the value of the farmer's work to himself, and until
very recently few if any courses in organic farming in American
agricultural schools. They are now in every such school. The
position of organic farming clashes at very many points with the
trends induced by agribusiness and their continuous expansion
of individual acreages. There are very good reasons for a smaller
size of farm and the deeper personal attitudes that it invites.
We have also seen in the 1980s a fearful decimation of farms
simply because the price of land suddenly declined; and so did
the farmers' security with banks, who promptly foreclosed them
for debts incurred in the expansion of acreage and machinery
which, now on the books, they were unable to pay when the
security was called in.

It is staggering to look at the farming success of the Amish, mostly on farms of from sixty to a hundred and twenty acres, a success acknowledged by non-Amish farmers almost everywhere. It is based on the fact that farming is highly prized enough among them as a way of life to encourage their young people to go into it, instead of being warned that any such idea is sentimental nonsense. In fact, because their religion forbids the use of motor-powered machinery in field work, an entire Amish industry has developed in very skillfully altering tractor tools for use with horses and constructing new horse-powered equipment.

As I look back, it is the color and drama of that American farm life that haunts my imagination. In the first place, the contrast with Ireland is very sharp. I had never seen anything remotely like the stockyards in Chicago, which Carl Sandburg was thinking of in the words "Hog butcher for the world." A young man like myself had seen Irish markets and fairs, amusing enough and full of cunning and cheating, when one was part of the inside of them, but their exterior was unimpressive—just village streets crowded with cattle and sheep held in corners and isolable spots by men and boys. And with the slow advance of would-be buyers with apparently endless bids, refusals, rebids, and final acceptance going on for hours, even the big Dublin market on the North Circular Road (as discussed in Joyce's *Ulysses*) was a collection of pens with buying and selling techniques very similar to the village fair. The auction rings of the continent, now all over Ireland and even then in much of America, did very little in the disposal of the vast numbers of cattle, sheep and hogs from all over the Midwest and brought to Chicago by rail and trucks in the forties. Every day of the week from Monday to Thursday in Chicago one would have in the yards ten to fifteen thousand cattle, five thousand sheep, and up to thirty thousand hogs. These animals were nearly all finished for slaughter and were being sold by commission men to factory officials. They were ranged in place over a huge acreage. Because of the size, the buyers all rode horses, and because this was America, they wore complete cowboy attire—boots, hats, and all. They rode up and down the pens and then when the agents of the commission firms stood waiting, a buyer would ride up and say, "What do you want on this bunch of cows" as he flicked one or two of the worn-out milk cows with his long whip. "Ten cents" would be the answer (cattle were always sold by the pound). "Is eight cents any good to you?" "Not now, Joe," was the answer. And "Then I'll look in on my way back" and off he cantered. The ethics of the buying and selling were very strict. If the man could get more than eight cents, he would, naturally. But the buyer was also absolutely bound by his eight-cent offer. He couldn't, as it was done again and again in Ireland at the time, reduce it to seven or six cents if later in the day the seller had not been able to get beyond the eight. On the seller's part, he dare not lie. He could not for instance tell the buyer that he already had nine cents unless he really had it. The buyers talked to one another and would find it out. If caught out in such a lie, the buyer would naturally appeal to the agency to punish the liar, and after two or three such incidents the seller lost his job. In the whole proceeding everything depended on an agreed case of truth-telling.

In a huge building at the center of the yards was a board with constantly changing radio reports outlining the top prices of all kinds of animals obtained in a series of other cities—Omaha, Kansas City, Buffalo, and the like. The mass of riders leaving their horses to be held outside and crowding in to look at the flashing screens were a blend of old and new in a utilitarian setting that was stunning to the like of me, especially when the utilitarian aspects of such a scene were charged with a conscious flamboyance, as in this case the dress. The yards are gone now, of course; their site in the city finally became too valuable not to be sold for development. But other cities still have markets substantially like the old one in Chicago, though I think never so outrageous in size or in atmosphere.

I was introduced to the yards by one of the most interesting men I met in Lemont, the little town and district in which my first farm was established. His name was Louis Jacobs (always pronounced "Louie"), a Lithuanian Jew who came to America (and to Lemont) in 1910. First he bought and peddled junk with a horse and cart, and then rose to regular transportation with a team of horses and wagon, and finally to two trucks for carrying livestock to the yards and doing a certain amount of dealing himself. He also rented any farm vacant for a while, getting someone unemployed (and usually slightly shady) to do the work until it was sold again. He had a little house in town and was himself funny and appealing in a very special sort of way. There was a convent in Lemont with a farm run by nuns with some male help, and they used Louis to do their trucking. He told me one day that Mother Superior had spoken to him and said, "Mr. Jacobs, I saw you last week trucking stock on a Sunday and that isn't right." "No," said Louis, "but you know, Sister, that isn't my Sabbath." "Ah, but Mr. Jacobs, I saw you trucking livestock on the day before."

He told me another event in his early days in the village. He brought his team to be shod by the blacksmith. The blacksmith was a very large and muscular German, who said, "We want no Jews here." Louis said, "You shoe horses for money. Why is the money from my horses no good to you?" I suppose something in the young Jew, slim but immensely tough, impressed the man, for he said, "Younker, I'll do a deal with you. We'll wrestle. If you win, I shoe your horse; if I win, out with you and don't come in here again." They wrestled and Louis won. He was, many years after, still immensely strong, though he never looked it exactly. The smith who shod his horses, when Louis offered him the money, said, "You don't owe me anything. The fight makes it quits, and then you can come in again if you like." Louis was a friend of the smith till the end of his days. The smith said to me one day, "Did you ever hear of how I came to meet Louis?" And he then recounted the whole story, word for word, as Louis had told it to me. Louis was friends with the man's sons and grandsons. I knew them all. One said to me once, "The best Jew I ever knew." In the yards he was invariably known as "the Jew from Lemont." I was introduced to Louis's favorite commission man, called Kelly. Kelly said, "You see the Jews and the Irish, we always get on well." And the reference was always made to a great Chicago shoe store called O'Connor and Goldberg.

It was no real surprise to me, living in Lemont in the 1940s, to hear of the much more open anti-Semitism of Louis's days in his home country. Even in the 1940s, Lemont was full of first- and second-generation Germans, and the anti-Semitism was also fairly explicit in the Polish and Lithuanian-derived people. These people had a long and bitter record of it in the countries from which their parents or grandparents came, and kept the inherited prejudices alive, especially since there were almost no Jews around to disprove or justify the prejudice. Louis won almost all of his detractors over—I think for two reasons. The first was, quite simply, his incurably cheerful and good-natured optimism. He believed entirely in the American dream; and his own life, until the last few years of it, gave him confidence. But the second reason was somehow different and more tangled. His father had been a small cattle dealer in Lithuania. Louis told me of anti-Semitism there that was hair-raising in comparison with anything Lemont would show. I think Louis had become quite sure that there would be no society without anti-Semitism. He didn't react to the blacksmith's dislike with any surprise. But he felt that in America if you were tough and hard-working you would always succeed. He was clearly pleased at the blacksmith's challenge to a personal contest. That was a chance which he regarded as both fun and different. And of course he was quite right. What he thought about America gave him a conviction that it was the individual that really counted, that if you fought well (as in the deal with the blacksmith) or if you drove fair bargains and got rich in a regular way without help and without annoying people too much, Americans would finally think of you as one of themselves and either forget or downgrade all the traditional ill will toward Jews with which their particular national affiliations had loaded them. He was so good-humored and so secure that jokes about (and frequently against) the Jews which his associates, now genuinely new friends, still would throw at him left him quite undisturbed. He very often jokingly played his alleged Jewish role to the life. It all seemed to me admirable.

In the last few years of his life, he lost much of his modest little fortune through trusting a thoroughly stupid brother-in-law named Morris who wanted to set up a slaughterhouse and processing plant in Lemont to avoid the taxation and labor cost of the city. This man was a kosher veal butcher. He underestimated the cost of building, and the building of the factory staggered and was not completed for a year or two. Worst of all, the brother-in-law, used to buying calves in the yards by bargaining for a price per pound, had been rendered quite safe in his deals because the scale was at the end of the corridor and the calf's weight was there to be seen. But when Morris went around the country and tried to buy calves on site, it turned out that he was entirely unable to guess weights at all. He could miss the weight of the calf by as much as thirty or forty pounds, and his buying proved a complete disaster. The money Louis had lent him vanished and never reappeared. Louis retained just enough to live out his life with relations in the city, his wife having died—as I really believe, out of despair, because it was her brother who had destroyed Louis's fortune.

One last Louis story, a funny and a touching one. I went to Europe on a six-month sabbatical in 1950, and needed someone to run the farm in America for me. Of all odd choices the one I made was the weirdest. Allan Bloom, my then beginning graduate student, later so famous—author of *The Closing of the American Mind*—was chronically hard up and, poor chap, thought that he would really like living in Lemont with a car that carried him to Chicago for his university work. That winter was famous for its cold and snow. Allan ran out of money and eventually ate up all my chickens and ducks, but he looked after the sheep all right, and, most importantly, managed to survive himself in the cold of what must have been one of the worst winters ever. Later, to my great pleasure and a little to my surprise, I found he had won golden opinions from all the neighbors, and that they genuinely liked him—though this was not at all a hard thing to do. Among other connections he got to know Louis and his wife well, and took over my job of making out Louis's income tax for him (Louis couldn't read or write when he came to America and had never learned, though he spoke Yiddish, German, Polish, and Latvian). When I returned, Mrs. Jacobs, who never liked me as Louis did, said to me, "Don't get me wrong, but you must see that I would be glad to have a nice Jewish boy do our taxes." Louis at once said, "All right; but I trust Dave as much as any Jew I've ever known."

PLOWING

Of all the farm operations in which I have taken part, my favorite is plowing—and with horses. Even a tractor, instead of a team, does not destroy the charm of that work, though it grievously lessens it. I have owned, at one time or another, three small or medium-sized farms, one in Illinois, one in Wicklow on the east coast of Ireland, and one, my present one, in Cavan in the northeast of Ireland. My plowing was restricted to the first two. In Cavan, the land is altogether too "heavy," as it is termed, that is, too wet, which means that you are unlikely to get it plowed and worked up for sowing without rain interfering and even less likely to get your grain harvested for the same reason. My last plowing venture was something out of the common. It was in India, where I plowed for an hour or two with a team of oxen, the only time in my life I have handled cattle as work animals. There is so much written nowadays about the drudgery of old-fashioned farming, drudgery from which mechanization has freed us. The fact is that during nearly all of my lifetime, most heavy farmwork was done by animals under man's supervision. It was not a matter of hard manual work at all—only the difference between having animals supply the power or an engine. And the union of man and animal in an elemental task such as turning the sod and sowing the seed is a power job comparable to the other great traditional tasks such as sailing a boat or making something of wood. Plowing with horses in America was never hard work. You sat on an iron seat above the plowshare. The setting of a hole in the ratchet controlled the depth of the plowing, and your three good horses and you moved steadily up and down the furrow and the earth turned turtle under you. There was about it all an ecstasy of its own and its own peace.

Of course there was, and still is, digging by hand in gardens and suchlike. And, in urban populations, there is still a fair share of people who like the occupation, thank God. But still the rhetoric continues, enforcing the conviction, now almost always acquired at second hand, that oil has saved them from drudgery. As though driving work animals was drudgery and driving the tractor was not; and caring for animals after the workday was drudgery, but filling the tractor or repairing it was not. Hobbies, sport, and pets are of course the preferred forms of spending one's activity and gaining pleasure. The delight in plowing and the partnership with animals in it is as old as Hesiod as he gives directions for the strength of the tree-formed plow ready to resist the power of the oxen as they struggle with a hard spot in the furrow, or in Aeschylus's *Prometheus*, who gave man work-animals to be his substitute in the heaviest toils. It is there in Breughel's picture of the fall of Icarus as the plowman follows his mule with the little wheel in the plow in front of him already invented to hold the plow effortlessly in place at the depth desired.

As long as one is young, it does not matter much whether you ride the plow, as one used to do in America (and the Amish still do) or walk behind it as in most of Europe, providing you have this little wheel. You are then free of the effort of holding the plow at a certain depth against the pull of the team. Indeed, if your horses are well trained enough, and the ground not too heavy, there is no need of the plowman behind the plow at all. I remember about thirty-five years ago in Normandy watching a boy plowing with his black Percherons, and walking alongside the horses that did not even have a rein. They were tied from bit to bit with a loose rope on the inside trace horse, which was used only when the boy was going to lead them home. When they came to the end of the furrow, he would tip up the plow (they used there a reversible plow exactly like a similar, much larger tractor plow today), shout firm commands to his team, and round the horses would go.

The beauty of those days of plowing was startling. I am thinking now particularly of the Wicklow farm. Our plowing was usually done in March or April, though sometimes also in fall or late winter, when the ground was not hard frozen. In a typically early spring day, one walked just fast enough to keep warm, and the gulls and the rooks followed in the furrow to pick up the worms,

David with his mare, Patsy, and her foal

and the sun would come breaking up the little touch of hoarfrost. I can still relive it and delight sharply, almost with pain at its loss, for I will never enjoy it again. There is no plowing to be done on my Cavan farm and rather less in Ireland every year anyway. Grain farming is beginning to be centered in the New World and in enormous units which make the use of very heavy machinery economic. Ireland is really best suited to a grazing system and the raising of livestock, and, if the general farming of the past is diminishing, it is at least more interesting to manage animals on a small farm than cultivate the featureless huge "fields" like those to be seen now even in England, near Cambridge.

Of course, the joy of horse-plowing depended largely on the quality and training of your team. Plowing is hard, but not extremely hard work for horses, as long as either the land is light or, if it is heavy, you have enough horses on your team to deal with it. I recently saw an Amish farmer plowing very heavy land with a single sixteen-inch plowshare and four horses ahead. No one was being unduly strained, man or horse. Plowing is preeminently a matter of the rhythmic engagement of strength, and rhythm is something horses are really attuned to.

I remember a mare of mine in Ireland whom I trained at two years old and kept till her last days at seventeen. I hunted her, drove her in the trap, even did a little show jumping with her and every kind of farmwork. But I think she loved plowing most of all. She was superb at it. Her name was Patsy, and she was a relatively light "half-bred" horse. She learned her plowing from a sour old work mare called Anne, a constantly disgruntled old lady, perpetually grumbling with flattened ears and not above nipping you if you came in front of her. But she, too, loved plowing and she was able to impart the mystery to Patsy. For the plow must move very slowly and steadily to keep the furrow even, and this particularly in Wicklow is a matter of trusted cooperation between man and horse. For in Wicklow, every arable field has stones, anything from small, sharp rocks weighing twenty pounds to monstrous instruments of destruction of a quarter-of-a-ton weight. Every Wicklow farmer is constantly at war with stones, hauling them out with picks and shovels or tractors or, as a last alternative, dynamiting them. These men will tell you only half in jest that the stones continually grow again. What happens is that gradually the topsoil gets thinner; some of it is moved to one side or blows away and another stone somewhere reveals itself.

Clearly, if your plowshare hits one of these things, especially the large ones, it snaps. (It is indeed equipped with a removable point, so that doesn't matter much, though it is a nuisance if it continues happening as it does with tractor plowing.) The horses move very slowly and are wonderfully aware when the stone is under their feet, at which point they stop before the plowshare hits it. Devoted old horsemen always say that they feel the stone, maybe six inches under the earth. I think that the sensitivity lies not directly in the feet but in an unusual awareness, a second or two before impact, that there is a slowness or unwillingness of the plowshare to make its way.

14

Riding to Hounds

It's a paradox that today's hunting—I mean the hunting of especially the fox, from horseback with a pack of hounds—should be especially blamed in the press and public opinion even to the forming of demonstrations. For certainly today hunts kill fewer of the animals they hunt than ever before. I remember that thirty years ago I inquired of the kennel-huntsman of a famous midland hunt in Ireland how many foxes he usually accounted for in a season. He answered, "Including cub-hunting, about fifty or sixty couple." (The reckoning of the foxes killed and the number of hounds hunting is traditionally quoted in twos, as couples.) Cubbing is the early hunting in August or September of the spring-born cubs. This is done to leave alive only the toughest foxes who show agility and cunning in getting away. The others, failing in the attributes which make them worthwhile in the eyes of the huntsman, had better be killed. Otherwise they only increase the number of unpopular predators, making farmers angry and contemptuous of foxhunting as a means of diminishing the pests. In theory at least, and probably in fact, the foxes that survive are animals likely to give the hunt later a good day's sport and frequently live on to "improve" the breed of foxes. Today my kennel-huntsman of the same hunt would be compelled to answer with a much lower number.

There is unquestionably something disagreeably cold-blooded about such a calculation as to the numbers killed, but certainly some solid facts should be noted to qualify this impression. Foxes cannot possibly be allowed to multiply without control in farming regions anywhere. With every nonhunting method of keeping the foxes down, foxes are nonetheless never eliminated. For instance, today they infest the outskirts of cities and live off the garbage bins in places like Liverpool. It is true that in their more natural habitats, their prey is largely mice, frogs, and rabbits; but it is also lambs, chickens, and ducks. They are immensely bold and their traditional cunning is true enough. If there is no hunting, especially in small countries like Ireland and Britain with large farming areas, the damage done by them is considerable and the frustration and anger of farmers far more than that. As a result, foxes are shot, trapped, poisoned, and gassed in their burrows. It is simply not arguable that any of these methods of killing them is less cruel than hunting. None of them is quicker or less painful. What turns most popular uninformed opinion against hunting is the feeling for a helpless creature driven to its death after hours of running by a pack of dogs, attended by a gaudy assembly of human beings in red or green or black fancy dress, all upper-class, stupid snobs: "The unspeakable in full pursuit of the uneatable." This is sentimental rubbish. The fox is a very curious, wily animal with an almost limitless desire to tease. I was once walking with a collie on my farm in Ireland and met with a fox. The dog took after him and immediately the fox took up the challenge. As soon as the dog got near him, the fox dodged, always successfully. He would then deliberately incite the dog to try again. The game went on for nearly ten minutes. The fox then simply left the dog after one of his rushes at his would-be victim, and disappeared. The much-derided apology by huntsmen that the fox enjoys being hunted is very nearly true. What makes a difference to this statement is that twenty-four hounds (twelve couple) is a different proposition from the fox faced with a single dog. If they can get near enough to him they will unquestionably kill him, for his dodging tactics do not then avail him. If they do get so close to him, the end is over in a matter of seconds. There are no missing shots that still wound, nor the obviously dreadful sufferings in trapping, nor the ghastliness of poisoning or gassing. Until a very short period before this last phase, the fox will trot along, not very fast and not at all in desperation, keeping an adequate distance between himself and his pursuers. In American hunting, where the landscape is largely devoid of banks or hedges (common in Ireland), you can see the fox three or four times during the hunt. He is invariably keeping ahead of the hounds, just as I have described him. Because of his intelligence, which is much superior to that of the hounds, and his skill in availing of rivers and dung-marked cattle pastures, he escapes the hounds time and time again in the course of a hunt.

Which brings me back to my opening sentence. Today far fewer foxes are killed by hunting than ever before, just at the time when the anticruelty people are making the most fuss. Why is that? Well, first, because in most places and most countries there are fewer foxes, because there are more and more efficient farmers, and they have no hesitation at all in killing foxes by any and every means. And in all hunts I have known, the main—sometimes the only— enthusiasm for digging out a fox that has gone to ground after a chase has come from the local farmers. When the fox was dug out with a terrier and spades, he was either killed with a spade or thrown directly to the hounds, and the farmer normally made sure to see that this was actually done. All the same, I have on several occasions seen the huntsman connive at the escape of such a fox by elaborately withdrawing the hounds to "give the fox a chance," but really so that the initial dash of the fox would elude the hounds and their capacity to overtake him because of the roughness or other protection of the terrain. The huntsman does not want to finish off a fox that might give him another good day's sport; especially, as I remember in one case, if she is a vixen. The huntsman said to me, "we have hunted that vixen several times before, and she always raises a litter of three or four cubs each year."

This practice of digging out foxes with the aid of a terrier no longer exists; it is now forbidden by law.

So although the number of foxes has diminished, there is no denying that some of the sentimentality of the critics of hunting and their impact on popular opinion tells on both the huntsman and those who ride after him. There is nowadays guilt in the killing of any animal. The horrible cruelties of factory farming remain unnoticed by the consumers of pigs and poultry except to a minute extent. Slaughterhouses have been largely cleaned up, and the dispatch of cattle, sheep and pigs is often something much better on the score of cruelty than the death of men and women in hospitals, because it is shorn of sentimentality and is conceived in knowledge, practicality, and decision. The fact is that what we are guilty about is taking pleasure in a process involving the death of an animal, when we know more about the event itself than we do about either the life or the death of the creature that we ordinarily eat as meat. Such guilt existed even several hundred years ago: see the essay by Montaigne. See also the talk of "gallantry" applied to the fox in the talk of our grandfathers and great-grandfathers. This probably testifies that the sport as of then already had a moral face, and the moral face belonged to the victim. But there is certainly not the same feeling of guilt when divorced from the pleasure of pursuit. Even today there is a great deal less guilt expressed about shooting and fishing—I cannot exactly see why.

One further qualification: what I have said applies fully to fox-hunting only. Hare hunting is harder to justify, because a hare is such a very timid animal, and not a predator. If one wants to defend hare hunting—and I do want to defend all kinds of hunting within the meaning of the word as used in Great Britain—one must say first that hares are not inevitably killed. This is partly because when the hare has adopted the only tactic she knows, crouching down in the grass in her "form," and the hounds run past her as they very often do, there is always another hare in the next field to capture their attention. Most harrier packs chase a number of hares in a day's hunting, with very few fatal results. And most harriers also hunt foxes when they are in their territory, and sometimes for preference because of the greater challenge. As Somerville and Ross narrate in one of their RM stories, when some misguided Englishman expresses his wonder that the harrier pack he hunted with spent most of the day hunting a fox, his interlocutor remarks, "Sure, they whipped the hounds off hares."

(This "whipping off" of hounds involves more whip-cracking and shouting than bodily contact. Huntsmen are obviously not going to injure their hounds; but threat and force must be available in moments of crisis to prevent such catastrophes as the chasing and killing of farm animals.)

Stag hunting in Ireland is always the pursuit of a carted stag. The hunt owns and breeds deer. Only the stags are hunted and only when they are three to four years old. One of these is released from the paddock in which they customarily live and given half an hour's "law," which he utilizes to set the maximum distance between himself and the hounds. Meanwhile the truck belonging to the hunt follows carefully along the roads that border the lines of the chase, watching for the moment when the hunt is terminated; usually when the stag is brought to bay and the huntsman jumps off his horse, whips off the hounds, and with the help of a rope and various members of the field, takes the stag to the truck. He will probably run another day, but not before the interval of several months. An individual stag normally follows the same line of running, that is, the line he took the last time he was hunted. The truck waits in the road for the end of the hunt as I have described, to bring the stag home.

A friend of mine was once out hunting with the famous Ward Union staghounds. The hounds went too fast for my friend and he lost contact. As he tried to figure out his whereabouts, he came to a place in the road where the hunt truck was stationed. Hardly had he seen it and approached the driver to get information, when he saw the stag jump over the hedge and trot along the road toward the truck. The driver let down the ramp and the stag got in very happily. My friend said that the whole thing savored of a man anxiously waiting for a taxi.

Despite the undeniable efforts by the hunt and its members to make the true conclusion of a hunt as little sanguinary as possible, this in itself is only just a part of what should be said in defense of hunting. The death of an animal pursued by its natural enemies, even with man's skill aiding and abetting the hounds, is a mimic representation of a very old and elementary game—one might almost call it a ritual. Game, however, rather than ritual, because it is open in its consequence; it can result either way. The skill and scenting power of the hounds, the stamina and cleverness of the horses and their riders, the tenacity and cunning of the victim touch something basic in human history. There are not many such processes in present-day life. Plowing and sailing are such, but their elemental character is somewhat obscured by the mechanization of the means. The practice of deep-sea fishing and the risks absolutely inherent in it, the skill that can most times baffle the sea but not the final time, all belong in this category too. To my mind life becomes startlingly poorer, less colorful, less suggestive of truth if any of all these games or necessary arts diminish or vanish. They constitute the mimicry of moments of conquest and defeat in the archaic life of man. I do not think that it matters very much that in its modern practice it does not include some of its ancient cruelty, or at least only to an unavoidable degree. To suit our greater squeamishness, no bad thing in itself, we may modify the manner of the end. But this is very different from abolishing the whole game in the name of sweeping away every trace of its original violence. So drag hunting, that is the hounds following the scent of the fox's bed dragged by a man on a horse, is unsatisfactory simply because the element of unknowingness, the last trace of the openness of conclusion in the hunt, is removed. It then becomes no better and no worse than any other competition in riding and jumping. Hunting is far more than this.

I have hunted in Ireland and the United States; never in England, where perhaps the greatest hunting still exists, nor on the Continent, where the French version is exclusively stag hunting and, as I understand, involves no jumping, no regular cross-country riding, but is practiced over a territory of the rides in forests. In Germany, hunting consists only of drag hunts.

In Ireland and the United States the basic organization of a hunt is the same. It is a club with a definite territory which has remained fairly well fixed, and in Ireland has been set by the Master of Hunts Association within the last hundred or so years. The first foxhunts in England were led by James II, then Duke of York, in the last half of the seventeenth century. What is certainly one of the first hunts in Ireland is the Fermanagh Harriers, which was started about 1700 as both recreation and training exercise for the cavalry unit there, the Enniskillen Dragoons, and later turned into the active hunt club which it is today. In Ireland and in the United States the excellence of sport offered by a hunt is absolutely dependent on two factors—the personality of an autocratic master and the attitude of the farmers in the various areas where the hunt meets. In modern times the latter precondition of good hunting has to stand up to great strain. It is true that in modern Ireland a very small part of the land is in crops like winter wheat, and most of it is in permanent or semipermanent pasture; and therefore one might suppose that foxhunting, being conducted in the wintertime, would have a better chance in Ireland than elsewhere, since pasture is relatively undamaged by horses' hooves. But such pasture nowadays is very often sown grass, perhaps only two or three years old, and so is vulnerable to the hooves of between twenty and forty horsemen galloping over the land in wintertime after heavy rain, which may turn it into mud. Moreover, the charm of hunting in Ireland is largely that of jumping over "natural" obstacles such as stone walls, hedges, and banks, which themselves double both as fences for jumping and also as fences to keep livestock in. In the latter capacity they can also be ruined by careless or incompetent jumping. It is indeed a wonder that such huge allotments of hunting country are cheerfully allowed by those local farmers who grant them permission to hunt, to ride over their land between November and March. It is true that the master is an autocrat. Decisions about the order of "meets" and the conduct of the hunt are entirely his; but he must also be a benevolent and popular autocrat in the district, and he must have a silver tongue and a ready hand to stand drinks in the local pubs, if the hunt is to persist and to show good sport. And the hunt must have a fund to draw on to cover comparatively small losses caused by foxes to poultry and not-so-small losses to lambs. Hunting must pay for these or somehow avoid them, or else foxes will be heavily reduced in number by shooting or poison.

American hunting is basically the same, but there are certain minor differences that matter. In the first place very few American hunts have much natural country at their disposal. They hunt over large, open fields exclusively fenced with barbed wire, and if the horses are going to cross these, "chicken coops" so called, three and a half to four feet high and built of wood, are hinged over the fences at one place in the field that would be easiest to take. As a result, the hunt always resolves itself into a number of small or large queues of followers. This in itself is a little tame in comparison with taking your own line, which is pretty common in Ireland. Furthermore, because the jumps are always the same and not very high, horses get careless and tend to trail their hind legs. As the chicken coop is fixed immovably, the result is frequently a very severe fall for both horse and rider, which those who have not joined in American hunting would not expect, since the obstacles are not at all demanding.

Another unfortunate difference is that although most American hunts are in theory and even in practice democratic in membership, the fees are high and not many of those who ride are other than rich. This makes it at times a rich man's club mostly consisting of wealthy businesspeople, some retired military officers, and the occasional wealthy farmer. By contrast, Irish hunts often consist 80 percent of farmers, and many of the riders are farmers' sons or daughters of eighteen to twenty breaking in their young horses themselves; and they are often attired in thoroughly unconventional clothes, wearing Wellington boots instead of proper riding equipment. So the farmers who own land assigned to an Irish hunt are more likely to see the whole thing more tolerantly, if not with enthusiasm, even allowing for the kind of modern exceptions I have mentioned.

The greatest single advantage American hunting has over Irish is the great ease with which one can see the fox so very often in a hunt, watch what he is doing and where he is going, and consequently get to understand far more of the skill of hounds in following him. I certainly learnt this almost altogether in America, and this is perhaps theoretically the most interesting aspect of the hunt.

I remember some funny incidents involving the masters of several hunts with which I have hunted. The master of one in Ireland, an extraordinarily intrepid rider, would always try to lose his "field" (i.e., other riders) at various moments of the day's sport, but especially at the beginning of the day. He would reappear and inevitably comment, "Where were you all? I was there all on my own and had the best run in three seasons. There was nothing to stand in your way. That hedge is big, but you can see through it and the barbed wire is only up to three foot of it. Otherwise, there was nothing but that bank with the water both sides of it, and any horse used in this district should make nothing of that." It is true that this master's hounds always ran brilliantly—that is to say they would get away, hot on the scent, far more than almost any pack, because their loving master never tried to control them.

At the other end of the scale was a master who hunted a very nice bit of country and was very popular with the farmers and his field but felt it necessary to have the most exaggerated discipline over his pack. He would ride well but perhaps a trifle too discreetly—though not too much should be said on that score, as I hunted with him till he was almost seventy—but at the least hint that we were entering fields where there were sheep, he would blow his horn and call off his hounds. They invariably came trotting back, leaving a fresh line of scent—so absolutely did they see their sense of duty to Al McGuinness. I know that the technical side of hunting owes far more to the likes of the first master, but the second master also made great contributions to farmers' goodwill toward hunting, and I have also enjoyed many excellent days behind him—pretty well as many as with the first.

Not every horse, not even every good horse, can fulfill the needs of a master of hounds. The master must automatically lead the field, unless he personally tells someone else to do so; this means that his horse must be the first to face every jump without the encouragement which all horses feel at following another horse ahead of them. The master must know his way across every field in his country, and where the fences prove impossible and must be avoided, how to find another way around them. Since hunts in Ireland have a relatively large territory, and rarely hunt more than twice in one location during a season, a master has to have intimate knowledge of literally miles and miles of country. And of the dispositions of the owners of the area and how not to offend them, and if you do, how to conciliate them.

All in all, hunting is something entirely on its own. For enjoyment and revealing yourself to yourself it hasn't its equal. Trollope says somewhere that he believes three-quarters of the field of riders in any hunt are frightened to death half of the time. He's probably right. But it is a very great thing to have your enjoyment so combined with the sense of being on your mettle, which naturally involves being frightened. Between this aspect and the primitiveness of hunting it seems to me that there is no sport and certainly no game that can hold a candle to it. Long may it flourish—and I believe it will.

Epilogue

WHO HE WAS

David Grene wrote these memoirs between 1993 and 2002. What he did not include were discussions of his personal life regarding his two marriages, his children, and other close associations, which he decided could be painful for some of those involved. He died on September 10, 2002, at the age of eighty-nine, and two days later a small memorial service was held for him in Bond Chapel on the campus of the University of Chicago.

The following pages begin with an article about him in the book *University of Chicago*, followed by some things that were said at the memorial service and in an Internet write-up by a student, and an obituary in his local Irish newspaper.

The memoirs are David's account of himself and what he saw. These pages complete the story.

Ethel Grene
(David's wife)

EDWARD ROSENHEIM
(Professor of English, University of Chicago)

David Grene was a teacher of enormous importance. There is so much colorful anecdote surrounding this indelibly Irish classicist—his farm and its livestock, his horsemanship, his gifted offspring, his travels, his friends and enemies, his habits of dressing, lecturing, and socializing, his own anecdotes, his convictions on all imaginable issues—that there is some danger of slighting the central, prodigious gift he has brought to the university for more than fifty years. That gift was clear, at the outset, to the teenaged students who sat in the twenty-five-year-old Grene's classes. It was the gift of a learning so wide and profound yet accessible that—delighted though we often were by the brilliance of his neckties and his metaphors, or by the bits of horse dung that fell from his boots as he paced about the lecture room—we were never really diverted from our encounter with texts and contexts and the problems and pleasures attaching to them.

If it is good to be welcomed to a community of scholars, it is even more gratifying to be talked to as a peer by a brilliant, intense, but amusing man who seems to assume that his students share his mastery of Greek, Latin, French, and German, and who acts as though, together, we are all simply refreshing our knowledge of the *Republic,* the *Oresteia, The Tempest,* the *Leviathan,* or *Ulysses.* I think I speak for many of his students when I say that we honor him above all as a man deeply, naturally, and confidently involved in a universe of books and ideas, who cheerfully assumed that we were, too.

KERI ELIZABETH AMES

David knew Greek like no one else; it was as close to a native language in him as a dead language can get. When he objected to a Homeric translation, he always talked as if he had just returned from having a martini at Jimmy's pub with Homer and was thus the most epistemically authoritative person alive. And so in fact he was. Much of being his student in Greek required yielding to the terror of following one's own intuition in David's presence, of trying to learn Greek from the inside rather than like a code to be cracked. That was reading Greek with David, where people like Amirthanayagam could read anything at sight and I could read only a few lines in the beginning, and yet David taught us all alike, with the same fervor and the same certainty that any of us might disclose to him some wonderful epiphany which had eluded him on every previous reading in the last seventy years.

GREGORY GRENE

... It is a different image that springs to my mind: the very particular hands, those large, ungainly, and completely forceful and lovable paws that my father had, stretched across the table to ask forgiveness of a sulky nine-year-old boy—me.

RUTH GRENE

... The father who raised me was a farmer by days, and a reader and explainer of plays, poems, and human nature in the evenings. We lived by books, the love of other cultures, living and dead, by milking the cows, by long long days in the fields during planting and harvest time, and trips to Dublin to see the occasional play or to go to the cattle market to pick out more cows for the herd. It was very exciting to stroll past the cows that were for sale at 5:30 of a damp and gray morning, and to listen to my father assessing them, in what seemed like a mystical way. The one that he picked out was invested by me with some indefinable quality...

"DAVID GRENE, 1913–2002," BY BEN DUEHOLM
(Internet article)

The farmer-classicist is a *rara avis* these days, and that is a shame—
Homer is far, far earthier than those who teach his poetry today.
There are probably now no professors left who can discourse on
the great performances of *Lear* in pre-*Anschluss* Vienna (I remember something like this: "Later he was tried for war crimes—a
very bad man. But a great King Lear"). Part of his appeal as a
teacher last year was his anachronistic quality. When he taught
T. S. Eliot or Yeats, he was teaching his contemporaries—and in
the case of Eliot, a former colleague.

    . . . For me, he was the coteacher of the two best classes of
my undergraduate career, one on Eliot's *Four Quartets* and the
other on *The Tempest*. He read Eliot far better than Eliot himself,
and he had a singular gift for Shakespeare's language, knowing
intuitively when to reverse feet, and how to stress the crucial
"if" in Miranda's first lines. It is too fitting, painfully fitting, that
the last two courses of his career should have been on great
poets confronting mortality and renouncing their craft, but even
without this unfortunate denouement, I would have found him
unforgettable.

"DISTINGUISHED GREEK SCHOLAR LAID TO REST,"
BY P. J. KENNEDY
(From the *Anglo-Celt* newspaper obituary)

Professor David Grene died after a short illness in Chicago, USA, on September 10th. The Professor of Greek literature lectured on the great texts in universities such as Trinity, Harvard, Vienna and for sixty-four years in the University of Chicago. His translations of the Greek tragedies have sold worldwide. Among his many eminent students were Joseph Frank, the Russian Literary expert, and Allan Bloom, political theorist at the University of Chicago.

Undoubtedly, it was as a farmer and obliging neighbor in Derrycark, Belturbet, that Professor Grene is surely remembered here. His farmyard teemed with fowl. David kept a few sows; he always appreciated their value as an extra income on his Derrycark holding. His fourteen cows were a picture. He was a loyal milk supplier to Belturbet and Killeshandra creamery.

David Grene was an expert horseman and this was often evident at Belturbet Agricultural Show. He trained horses for hunting and for working in carts, traps, hay machinery and plowing. He regularly traveled on horseback to bring home his cows for milking.

The funeral service was conducted by Archdeacon Johnston, who on behalf of the family invited the congregation back to their house, where the neighbors had the tea wet and the buns buttered in the tree-veiled front garden facing the byre where he milked his cows.

Recording from Othello

A recording of a remarkable reading by David Grene of the final scene of Shakespeare's *Othello* is available in two ways:

- You can hear it on the Web site davidgrene.org.
- You can also order a CD at cost for $3.00 (three dollars) from a link on that Web site, or write to order it (with check enclosed) to

Fairfield Books
P.O. Box 8085
Wilmette, IL 60091

Select Bibliography

Works by David Grene

BOOKS

Man in His Pride: A Study in the Political Philosophy of Thucydides and Plato. Chicago: University of Chicago Press, 1950. Reprinted as *Greek Political Theory: The Image of Man in Thucydides and Plato*. Chicago: University of Chicago Press, 1965.

Reality and the Heroic Pattern: Last Plays of Ibsen, Shakespeare, and Sophocles. Chicago: University of Chicago Press, 1967.

The Actor in History: Studies in Shakespearean Stage Poetry. University Park: Pennsylvania State University Press, 1988.

TRANSLATIONS

Three Greek Tragedies in Translation. Chicago: University of Chicago Press, 1942.

The Complete Greek Tragedies. Edited with Richmond Lattimore. Chicago: University of Chicago Press, 1952–64.

Aeschylus:	*Seven against Thebes*	(1956)
	Prometheus Bound	(1942)
Sophocles:	*Oedipus Rex*	(1942)
	Electra	(1957)
	Philoctetes	(1957)
	Antigone	(1991)
	Oedipus at Colonus	(1991)
Euripides:	*Hippolytus*	(1955)

Herodotus, *The History*. Chicago: University of Chicago Press, 1988.

Aeschylus, *The Oresteia*. Translated with Wendy Doniger O'Flaherty. Chicago: University of Chicago Press, 1989.

Hesiod, *Works and Days*. In Stephanie A. Nelson, *God and the Land: The Metaphysics of Farming in Hesiod and Vergil with a Translation of Hesiod's* Works and Days *by David Grene*. New York: Oxford University Press, 1998.

EDITED WORKS

The Authoress of the Odyssey, by Samuel Butler, with an introduction by David Grene. Chicago: University of Chicago Press, 1967.

The Peloponnesian War, translated by Thomas Hobbes. Ann Arbor: University of Michigan Press, 1959. Reprint, Chicago: University of Chicago Press, 1989, with introduction by David Grene.

ARTICLES

"*Calidus inventa* (The Nurse's Speech, *Romeo and Juliet*)." *Hermathena* 47 (1932): 281.

"The Comic Technique of Aristophanes." *Hermathena* 50 (1937): 87–125.

"The Interpretation of the *Hippolytus* of Euripides." *Classical Philology* 34 (1939): 45–58.

"Method and Doctrine in Plato and Aristotle." *Transactions of the American Philological Association* 71 (1940): xxxvi–xxxvii.

"Prometheus Bound." *Classical Philology* 35 (1940): 22–38.

"Herodotus: The Historian as Dramatist." *Journal of Philosophy* 58.18 (1961): 477–88.

Introduction to *Most Ancient Verse*. Edited by Thorkild Jakobsen and John A. Wilson. Chicago: University of Chicago Press, 1963.

"Chance and Pity." *Midway* 27 (1966): 79–91.

"The Strangest Work of Classical Scholarship: Samuel Butler's *The Authoress of the Odyssey*." *Midway* 8 (1967): 69–79.

"The *Odyssey:* An Approach." *Midway* 9 (1969): 47–68.

"Aeschylus: Myth, Religion, and Poetry." *History of Religions* 23 (1983): 1–17.

"On the Rarity Value of Translations from the Greek." *Journal of General Education* 39.2 (1987): 69–76.

"Hesiod: Religion and Poetry in the *Works and Days*." In *Radical Pluralism and Truth: David Tracy and the Hermeneutics of Religion*, edited by Werner G. Jeanrond and Jennifer L. Rilke, 142–58. New York: Crossroad, 1991.

"Response" to Stephanie Nelson's "Justice and Farming in the *Works and Days*." In *The Greeks and Us: Essays in Honor of Arthur W. H. Adkins*, edited by R. Louden and P. Schollmeier, 36–42. Chicago: University of Chicago Press, 1996.